MAR

MARGINAL

PLANTS

BERNARD SLEEMAN

GUILD OF MASTER CRAFTSMAN PUBLICATIONS

First published 2002 by
Guild of Master Craftsman Publications Ltd,
166 High Street, Lewes,
East Sussex, BN7 1XU

ISBN 1 86108 256 8

A catalogue record of this book is available from the British Library

All photographs supplied by Harry Smith Horticultural Photographic
Collection except:
A–Z Botanical Collection Ltd., p 76
Ed Gabriel, pp vi, 2, 14, 17 and 30
Martin Page, pp 39, 50, 62, 69 and 108
Eric Sawford, pp 34 and 83
Bernard Sleeman, pp 35, 41, 42, 43, 63, 64, 71, 74, 78, 79, 85, 93, 94, 103 and 107

Illustrations by John Yates

Designed by Mind's Eye Design, Lewes
Cover design by Mind's Eye Design, Lewes
Typeface: Sabon and La Gioconda

Colour origination by Viscan Graphics (Singap[ ]
Printed and bound by Kyodo Printing (Singap[ ]
MRM Graphics, Winslow, Buckinghamshire, [ ]

CONTENTS

INTRODUCTION

Welcome to this book on marginal pond plants. In it I will pass on all the information you need to get your pond planting right first time and to propagate your own plants successfully. If you have problems with existing plants dying or just looking sick, you will also find how to make them thrive. Needless to say, I am aware of some of the frustrations suffered by both experienced pond owners and beginners. Therefore, my aim is to lay bare the mysteries and foibles of marginal plants and make pondkeeping even more fun.

At the end of the day you will see it is all common sense, often with more than a bit of hindsight, and I have no doubt many of you will say 'why didn't I think of that?'. It is simple, but how many of us look and really see? We all tend to take many things for granted, particularly so with nature. When you are next by a river, lake or stream, take a long hard look at where the marginal plants are actually growing and compare this with where the plants are situated in and around your pond.

One note of caution – please do not take plants from the wild: firstly, you will be breaking the law and secondly, by doing so you will, without a doubt, import a considerable variety of unwanted bugs into your pond. Fish lice, one example, are particularly difficult to eradicate. These parasites burrow in between the scales of fish where they feed off their body fluids. More often than not, their presence won't be obvious until you have a heavy infestation, by which time it will be difficult to eradicate and the fish will be flicking themselves against any hard object, trying to remove the irritants.

There are really just a few basic factors that have a marked effect upon a plant's health and upon the health of the pond. All have a bearing on the pocket too; the more aware you are of your pond plant's needs, the less you will waste and the more you'll save.

Chapters 1, 2 and 3 cover the basic needs of pond plants, Chapter 4 covers propagation techniques, and the Directory – Adding Interest: Happy Plants – covers individual plants in detail. By no means does this book include all of the plants that are suitable for pond use, but it does cover what tend to be the most popular, and useful, genera and varieties.

MAINTAINING THE BALANCE

A HEALTHY POND

❧

Plant life and pond ecology

❧

Water and soil requirements

❧

Pests and diseases

❧

Propagation

❧

CHAPTER I

PLANT LIFE AND POND ECOLOGY

Often used to describe, en block, all the plants grown in and around the edge of a pond, 'marginal pond plants' is a common phrase, but what is a marginal plant? Very loosely, it is a plant that has evolved to grow at varying levels, or zones, around the edges of lakes, rivers, streams and ponds. Essentially it is a marsh plant, growing in the margin between dry ground and the water's edge – an area that is usually subject to occasional flooding. Given this situation, marginal plants have evolved to cope with a fair range of conditions, to the pondkeeper's benefit, but only a relative few will grow happily when fully submerged.

Marginal plants grow at various levels in and around the water's edge

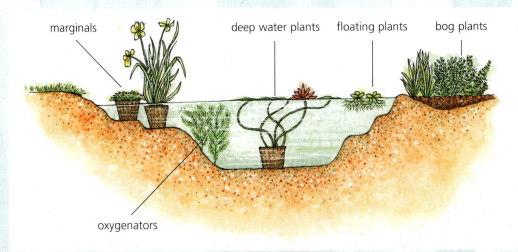

marginals · deep water plants · floating plants · bog plants

oxygenators

NATURAL PONDS

Why do you never see a natural lake, pond or stream – one that has not been polluted – in poor condition, full of slime and pea green? The short, simple answer is that plant life, in a natural environment, will develop in balance with the volume of water and the number of fish, frogs and other species that live within its confines. It is an environment which, if left to its own devices, will keep itself in balance. Only when man 'lends a hand' do things go awry.

What maintains this natural balance? All the fauna in a pond, from snail to fish, excrete waste material. This waste is gradually broken down into plant food through the biological processes illustrated in the chart on p 7, and this broken-down waste is then used by plants to fuel the continued growth of their foliage. This, in turn, produces oxygen, a positive contribution to the environment. A careful look at the submerged root systems of plants around natural lakes and ponds will reveal what we call aerial roots. These extend out into the water rather than being buried in the soil, thus helping marginal plants to consume the converted waste material and keep the water clean. The bacteria responsible for the conversion of animal wastes into plant food will be present in numbers directly proportional to the amount of waste produced, and because they multiply only very slowly, they cannot cope with any sudden increase in the amount of waste produced. The sudden introduction of large numbers of fish would throw the system out of balance; there would be some fatalities and all of the fish would suffer.

aerial roots

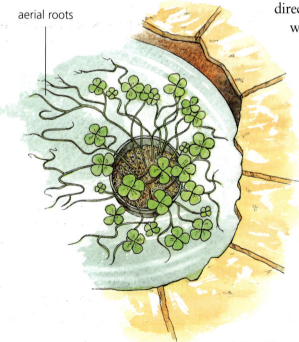

Aerial roots increase the transfer of waste and nutrients between plants and the surrounding water

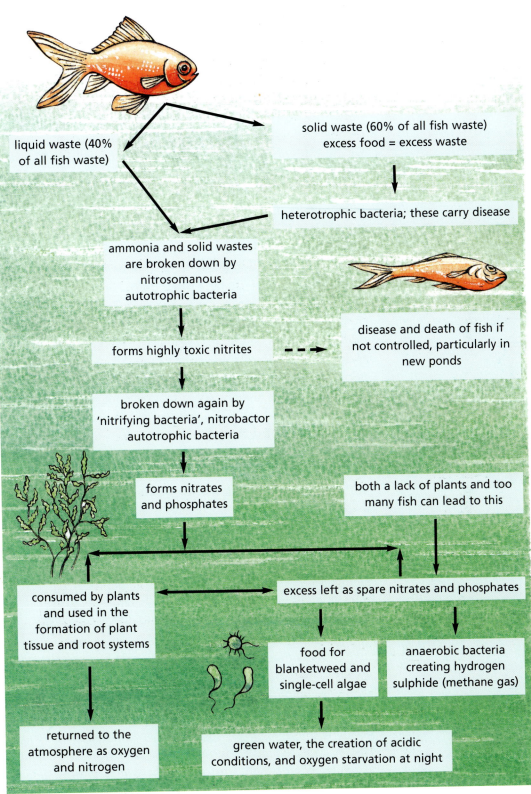

liquid waste (40% of all fish waste)

solid waste (60% of all fish waste)
excess food = excess waste

heterotrophic bacteria; these carry disease

ammonia and solid wastes are broken down by nitrosomanous autotrophic bacteria

forms highly toxic nitrites

disease and death of fish if not controlled, particularly in new ponds

broken down again by 'nitrifying bacteria', nitrobactor autotrophic bacteria

forms nitrates and phosphates

both a lack of plants and too many fish can lead to this

consumed by plants and used in the formation of plant tissue and root systems

excess left as spare nitrates and phosphates

food for blanketweed and single-cell algae

anaerobic bacteria creating hydrogen sulphide (methane gas)

returned to the atmosphere as oxygen and nitrogen

green water, the creation of acidic conditions, and oxygen starvation at night

The pond cycle works to maintain the ecological balance of the natural environment

MAN-MADE PONDS

A garden pond is, in effect, a micro-environment in which we are attempting to re-create, on a much smaller scale, that which mother nature has taken millions of years to perfect. We often add fish in numbers far greater than the pond can support. The greater the number of fish, the greater the volume of plant food produced and the greater the number of plants required to maintain the pond's ecological balance. A pond is not like a cage; you cannot take a broom to it every few days to clean it out. It is reliant upon the biological processes that have evolved to fulfil this task, and must be self-sustaining. Marginal plants have evolved to do the cleaning job in water-based habitats; they consume the resultant 'soup' of biologically reduced fish waste. However, as a garden pond is man-made, these processes are subject to abuse and miscalculation – the overriding reason for almost all of the problems a pondkeeper will encounter. You must consider how many plants you will need to consume the waste produced by the number of fish you want to introduce.

POND FLORA

When it comes to a healthy pond, variety is the spice of life. You need a good range of plants to constantly consume the nitrates (plant food) that are in suspension – a by-product of the biological processes occurring in the pond. These need to be consumed at a steady rate throughout the spring, summer, autumn and, to a lesser extent, winter, so you need plants that will be at their most vigorous at varying times in order to maintain an even balance year-round.

If all marginals flowered at the same time there wouldn't be enough plant food to support them and after a short while they would suffer. Conversely, if they all stopped feeding at the same time, our pond would soon turn a beautiful pea green and maybe even start to smell. Consequently, plants have evolved to flourish over the spring, summer and early autumn, almost certainly by filling niches found within those seasons. Some varieties, though relatively few, even carry on growing, albeit slowly, throughout the winter. During the colder, shorter days of winter, the fauna in a pond eat less and thus produce less waste, so the balance is maintained.

The flowering time of a plant indicates when it is at its peak. To gauge the seasonal vigour of a plant, look at the month in which it flowers, the two or three months leading up to that, and the month after – this is usually its best growing period.

POND FAUNA

To obtain a balance within our micro-environment, we need to emulate nature and vary the type of plant we put in our pond. At the same time we must take care not to overload the pond with fish, exceeding its capacity to maintain this balance. It is very easy, and quite natural to do this as we all love the colour and movement of fish. How many times do people say 'just one more won't hurt', forgetting the straw that can break the camel's back?

If too many fish are added at one time they, and the pond's original inhabitants, could well suffer fatalities a couple of weeks later. Within hours of adding any more than two fish, the pond, albeit temporarily, will have become toxic. Because the bacteria in the pond cannot multiply quickly enough to cope with the sudden additional waste material being produced, an excess of ammonia and nitrites rapidly builds up. This phenomenon is known as new pond syndrome. The degree of toxicity and the time it takes to develop both depend upon the size of the pond, the size of the fish added and the overall inches of fish per square foot now in the pond. This toxicity has a dramatic effect on the ability of the fish to breathe, causing them to become ill. It will last only a few days at most – until the bacterial levels catch up with the levels of waste products – but the damage will have been done. Caution and patience are the watchwords. Add fish one or two at a time and do not overcrowd your pond.

It is unfortunate that the effects of toxicity generally only become noticeable a week or two after the event – in many cases this is too late. All pondkeepers should, at the very least, possess a nitrite test kit and use it to check their ponds regularly. When you add fish, use it at least once a day for the first week. This will help you avoid potentially serious problems: if you know something is going on, you are in a position to rectify it.

9

ALGAE

The prime causes of death and disease within a pond can be avoided if you study the natural environment and take on the lessons learnt. 'Dis-ease' is avoidable, and providing correct amounts of plant life in the right conditions, balanced with the pond fauna, is a major part of the commonsense care cycle. Even with sufficient bacterial levels to break down the waste in a pond, if there are too few plants, this converted waste will remain in the water, enabling algae to thrive. The result is pea soup; green water or, worse, blanketweed, with masses of thread-like algae covering the submerged parts of the plants. Green water is a highly visible indication that all is not well in your pond, that an imbalance exists. Algae will only thrive if there is an excess of plant food. If plant food is used by 'desirable' plants as it becomes available, algae cannot survive. It will be starved out of existence and your pond will remain clean, clear and healthy.

When a pond produces more waste than it can convert, green water is the visible result

A covering of blanket-weed is a clear indication that all is not well

ALGICIDES

A frequent mistake with pond care is the use of algicides. These will attack and kill off algae successfully, but do have negative side-effects. The plants in the pond will also absorb the algicide, resulting in retarded growth or even death. Water lilies and other submerged plants tend to be particularly susceptible.

Another factor to be considered is that, if the algae you have thus killed is not removed, it will fall to the bottom of the pond and decay, absorbing oxygen and giving off noxious, sometimes toxic gasses in the process.

Maintaining the balance

As you can see, a healthy pond is all a matter of balance. If you get it wrong and upset any part of the equation, problems will arise. At one end you have fauna producing waste, in the middle you have bacteria breaking this down and, at the other end, plants consuming the final product. Indicators of any imbalance are there for you to recognize, you just need to know what they are and what they tell you.

Never forget that a problem is usually the end result of a simple mistake made days, weeks or months earlier. Quick fixes usually have drawbacks and, more often than not, will not treat the cause of the problem. It is far better to find why a problem has arisen and fix this so that it does not happen again.

Guidelines

❧ Make sure you have the equivalent of one medium-sized plant for every 30cm (12in) of the pond's circumference.

❧ Include the equivalent of one-third the volume of the pond in submerged plants.

❧ Cover one-half to two-thirds of the surface of the pond with plants such as water lilies. Try to avoid most of the free-floating plants such as duckweed and Azolla spp.: they grow far too rapidly and often do more harm than good. They are also extremely difficult to get rid of once you have them, and can be a major source of pollution on the pond floor when they die off.

❧ Be careful not to let oxygenating plants take over. If there are too many, the fish will be gasping to breathe on hot summer nights. This is because plants reverse their cycle at night and give off carbon dioxide rather than oxygen.

❧ Do not exceed 25mm (1in) of fish to every 900 sq cm (1 sq ft).

CHAPTER 2

WATER AND SOIL REQUIREMENTS

Marginal plants are all different, and with good cause: if they all liked or needed the same conditions, it would lead to overcrowding and the failure of less vigorous or robust varieties – not what nature intended. In addition to knowing in what depth of water a plant would prefer to live, you need also to bear in mind what each plant prefers in the way of soil conditions. These two basic factors also have a considerable effect on the overall health of your pond: the happier a plant, the better it will grow and the more 'work' it will do to maintain the ecology of the pond.

WATER CONDITIONS

Some plants have evolved to take the occasional ducking whilst others will grow quite happily submerged in 20–30cm (10–12in) of water. Some plants used as marginals are terrestrial plants that aquatic nurserymen have found will tolerate, or even enjoy, very moist or wet conditions. Others are marsh or bog plants that have been found to grow well used as marginals. You need to differentiate between marginal and aquatic, as the true aquatic plants are the only ones that should be grown completely underwater. True aquatics are limited in number and variety. Other genera are required to pad out what is available, and will give you a more colourful and attractive pond as a result.

How a plant will cope with having its crown submerged for long periods varies widely according to the habitat in which it has evolved. Some marginals will grow better in a wetter environment – the true aquatics – while others prefer the drier side of the 'margin'. Knowing which is which, across the board, is the real key to success. I have noted all these considerations in the Directory (see the individual 'Ideal conditions' entries).

Use a combination of true aquatics and moisture-loving 'terrestrials' to create a lush water garden

As some readers will have found, to their cost, there are quite a few marginals that curl up their roots and die if you plant them in water that is too deep. More terrestrial than truly aquatic, their crown must be able to breathe or the plant will rot. Some like their whole root system in the water, others just the tips of the roots. The latter tends to be the case with some of the adopted, normally terrestrial marginals, where some care is needed.

What you will also find is that almost all marginals will grow 'dry', that is, with only the bottom of the pot in water. This is because all plants have developed mechanisms to help them survive a limited period of dehydration. Of course, if a plant becomes too dry it may well die, especially if it remains very dry for a long period.

Most growers exploit this ability of a plant to survive partial dehydration. It enables them to mass produce a wide range of marginal plants in a non-pond situation, in lightweight potting mediums. Being comparatively light, the resultant plants can be moved around relatively easily and cheaply. This is a trait you can use to good effect when propagating your own plants (see individual entries in the Directory).

SOIL CONDITIONS

The wetland habitats that marginal plants have evolved in all have a certain type of soil, which is similar worldwide. We frequently plonk our pond plants into a different medium or habitat – often both – and expect them to grow as well as they do in their natural setting.

Rather than placing plants in the pond in whatever medium they were sold, take the time to think about where they evolved and thus what their preferred growing medium is. The optimum soil conditions for most pond plants lean towards the neutral or even alkaline. What is particularly noticeable about the soil type you find around most lakes, rivers and streams is that it is always either clay or very heavy soil. This is what gives it the ability to hold water and what prevents it from washing away, as light soil or peat would.

Eriophorum angustifolium is the only marginal plant that prefers a peaty, acidic soil

As a consequence, all marginal plants, bar one of note – *Eriophorum angustifolium* (cotton grass) and this is really a bog plant – prefer heavy soil. As it is what they evolved in, what their root system has developed to thrive in, marginal plants will perform best in this type of growing medium. Even the more terrestrial plants prefer heavier soil when they are in a wet environment.

Peat

Some of you will have bought plants that began to look unwell, or maybe upped and died, a few weeks after planting. When you pulled them out of the pot did you notice a sulphurous smell? Plants in a planting medium consisting mainly of peat do not like being totally submerged. When peat is kept underwater, a chemical reaction occurs, resparking the continual breakdown of the peat that takes place when it is in its natural boggy environment. The sulphur dioxide you can smell is a by-product of this process; it retards and sometimes halts the plant's root growth. Try an experiment for yourself. Cut an existing plant, planted in a peat medium, down the middle. Repot one half using peat but wash all the peat off the other half and plant it up in heavy clay or soil. Use a little bone meal in each and place them side by side in the pond. Compare the plants after three months – you will see a clear difference.

As well as becoming a slowly decaying mass in water, peat is far too acidic for most plants. It is perfectly alright for garden use in reasonable quantities, particularly as buffers are always added to neutralize the inherent acidity of the peat. However, in water these buffers are soon dissolved and flushed away, returning the peat to its natural acidic state. Peat is also low in trace elements and natural nutrients and does not permit the slow movement of oxygenated water around the root system that a plant requires. The gasses it produces hinder this essential exchange, causing the slow death of the plant or, at best, leading to little or no growth. The wetter the conditions, the lower the peat content of the planting medium must be, fading to zero when a plant is to be fully submerged. Just think how acidic a pond would become if all the plants were in peat; this would also produce a totally unnatural situation for most aquatic fauna. A little acidity is fine but too much of anything is not good in a micro-environment.

Many growers use a peat-based medium. This is mainly out of necessity; a peat-based medium aids shipping and handling because it is relatively light – it weighs far less than clay – even when it is wet. This enables a greater number of plants to be moved at one time. Whilst many plants will tolerate and even grow quite well in this medium in 'dry' conditions, it is usually only the more vigorous varieties that will grow away and develop a root system, beyond the peat, in a pond environment. For the best results in your pond it is always wise to give the plant what it evolved in – good heavy loam or clay. As an added bonus, your plant is also more likely to stay standing up as this heavier medium in the planting container provides a stronger anchor.

Plants to be grown in the pond require a pot and planting medium that will provide a strong anchor

CHAPTER 3

PESTS AND DISEASES

Pests, in the form of various insects, pose a particular problem for many pondkeepers because, as a general rule, insecticides cannot be used in or around a pond environment. As a result, the usual way to try and rid marginal plants of bugs is to spray them off with a powerful jet from a hosepipe, letting the fish munch on the result. Failing that, if a plant is so badly infected that you are sure the only way to solve the problem is to spray with insecticide, remove the plant from the pond and isolate it before treating. Always use an insecticide that is bio-degradable; one that will break down harmlessly when it reaches soil. Keep the plant out of the pond until the infestation has completely cleared, and hose it off well before placing it back in the pond. The following paragraphs deal with the most common pests and diseases that affect marginal plants.

An infestation of woolly aphids

CHINA MARK MOTH LARVAE

The china mark moth lays its eggs on the underside of leaves. These eggs hatch out into cream worms, about 18–20mm (¾in) long, with a brown head and a distinctive brown line down their back. They can be found throughout the summer, both moving around and living in the flat cases they make by weaving a folded piece of leaf together with a silky substance they produce. They often make larger cases as they grow.

Drowning, by submerging the complete plant for an hour or so, is the only really effective way of dealing with this pest. Make sure the fish get all the larvae as they rise to the surface to escape.

CADDIS FLY

Caddis flies look like small moths but with one subtle difference; their wings are hairy rather than scaly. They lay their eggs near the water's edge, producing larvae, otherwise known as stick grubs, that live in the water in little shelters made of pond debris. These larvae can do a lot of damage to new flower buds, young growth and root systems, often biting right through them. If you find buds that have pieces missing, look for this little pest around the base of the plant. You can feed them to your larger fish but it is better to destroy them in case they escape from the smaller fish.

Fortunately, fast-moving fish usually see these little devils off before you even know you have them.

IRIS FLEA BEETLE

Around the middle of summer, these little beetles are more often in evidence than many would believe. They are bright blue, quite small and very active. They attack the leaves of iris and other suitably soft-leaved plants, leaving calling cards of small, longitudinal patches of leaf skeleton.

The only effective, safe way to deal with them is to remove the leaves and burn them as soon as you notice the beetles.

LEAF MINER

This pest is not something encountered every day but if you do see any, take care to ensure that you eradicate them all. There are two species you need to be aware of, and the tracks they leave on the leaf are often the only means of identifying which one you have: the flies themselves are not often seen. The most common species, *Liriomyza ranunculoides*, attacks soft-leaved plants, leaving a snaking trail of up to 5cm (2in) long and about as thick as a line from a broad-tipped ball-point pen. The second species, *L. hydrabensis*, leaves a much narrower trail, more like a fine thread. The fly of *L. hydrabensis* has an ochre brown spot on its back, that of *L. ranunculoides* does not.

If you find the very fine trails, or mines as they are called, of *L. hydrabensis* on your soft-leaved plants (calthas, ranunculus, and the like), remove the leaves immediately and seal them in a polythene bag, for eventual cremation. If it is still there, the larvae responsible for the damage will be at the fore end of the mine. As this species is a notifiable pest in many countries, you should inform the appropriate government authority and the centre from which you purchased the plant. If allowed to get out of hand, leaf miners can devastate salad crops.

IRIS SAWFLY

These pests are not often seen, but the results of their handiwork are very distinctive. Once again it is the larvae that do the damage. They munch away at the edges of leaves producing an almost serrated effect. Heavy infestations will cause leaves to die and rot. When they are fully grown the larvae pupate, drop down and burrow into the soil, to emerge the following spring.

The larvae are easy to spot – they look like small caterpillars – and can be picked off and fed to the fish. Liquid malathion is another very effective way of dealing with heavy infestations, but this should only be used in an isolated environment, well away from the pond.

WATER LILY APHID

These are the myriads of tiny black bugs often seen covering the leaves of water lilies. While these aphids have a particular penchant for the leaves of water lilies, if allowed to get out of hand, they will migrate to other, similarly juicy plants around the pond's circumference as the colony expands. They are more prevalent where there are plum and cherry trees in the vicinity of the pond, as these trees provide their favourite places to lay eggs and overwinter. The young, early summer hatchlings then fly to whatever food source is within reach, water lilies being one of their prime targets.

Regular hosing off, allowing the fish to feed on the aphids, is a simple form of control, and about the only one that can be used where fish are present. Heavily infested plants are difficult to clear and should be burnt, as should all leaves removed from infected plants.

WOOLLY APHID

Fortunately, woolly aphids are not common in aquatic plants, but they are very hard to dispose of once established. Colonies group together in little clusters at the base of plants, looking like small pieces of dirty cotton wool between the tightly packed stems and leaves. They suck out the very lifeblood of the plant – the sap – just as it is rising. Weak, floppy leaves are a sure sign that they are present.

They are virtually impervious to all but the strongest systemic insecticides and these, most being notifiable poisons, are best left to professional nurserymen. Drowning is another solution, but it is sometimes debatable as to which succumbs first – the plant or the aphids. By far the best treatment is to burn the whole plant, including the pot. That way you know you've got them all; leave just one and you will soon have a busy colony again.

DISEASES

Fortunately, there are few diseases that affect aquatic plants. The most noticeable is mildew. This appears on the old growth of all the calthas, being almost endemic in midsummer. Apart from being unsightly, it does no harm, and the simple remedy is to remove and burn any affected leaves.

Other diseases, such as rust and leaf spot, are usually the result of insect infestation; providing some care is taken with insect control few, if any, problems will arise. However, if they do, remove all the affected plants from the pond and treat them in isolation or, preferably, burn them.

21

CHAPTER 4

PROPAGATION

three-quarters fill a medium-size pot
(or seed tray) with seed compost and
sprinkle on the seeds

cover larger seeds, such as iris seeds,
with a 2mm (⅛in) layer of compost;
small seeds do not need covering

keep moist at all times, but not wet

Sowing seeds

smaller clumps of rushes and many other plants can be teased apart by loosening the root system; knock off most of the soil, push your thumbs into the centre of the root mass, and gently pull the two halves apart

replant as usual

Dividing roots by hand; use the same method for the division of crowns

large clumps of plants, such as *Cyperus longus*, need far more power to divide than hands can provide; push two forks down through the centre of the root mass and force them apart by pushing the handles away from each other. For very large clumps, do this several times

Dividing roots using two forks; tough crowns should be divided in the same way

this group includes mainly plants with an iris-type root system, and division is fairly easy to accomplish. Trace the multi-branched rhizome back to the main root and cut off 10cm (4in), including the plant you require. Small clumps can be pulled apart by hand; large clumps will require a knife

replant in the usual way, and keep moist at all times

trim the roots back to a manageable length

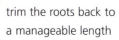

Dividing rhizomes

the root systems of plants such as *Ranunculus grandiflora* can be found sprawling all around the parent plant. Cut off a piece containing the growing tip and replant in wet soil. Take care: these fleshy roots are quite fragile and break very easily

remove about 10cm (4in) of young
growth from the parent plant

replant around the edge of a pot filled
with good soil. Keep the pot moist at
all times but not too wet: if it is too
wet, rotting may occur before the
cutting roots up

Propagating by stem cuttings

taking root cuttings from plants such as
Houttuynia cordata is simplicity itself.
Remove the plant from its container,
tease away the soil to expose the long,
trailing roots, and trim off several peices
about 10–12cm (4–5in) long

plant the cuttings up in a prepared pot and
cover with a light layer of soil. Keep moist and
not too wet. New plants will soon appear

plants such as sagittarias form new bulblets at the end of stoloniferous
roots. These can be found by removing the plant from its container
and easing away the soil. On plants in open-mesh, these bulblets will
frequently be exposed on the outside of the basket. Simply cut them
off, replant in good soil and replace in the pond

Dividing tubers

ADDING INTEREST

HAPPY PLANTS

There is little mystery involved in growing plants for your pond. All plants have similar behavioural characteristics when it comes to propagation. Seeds will germinate if the conditions are right. All we have to remember with marginal plants is that a little extra moisture is required. The only other difference we have to consider is that more aquatic than 'terrestrial' plants have inhibitors in their seed shell – to ensure the survival of the species. These inhibitors can vary from seed to seed, thereby ensuring full germination over several seasons, and enabling a species to cope with both drought and flood. In most cases sufficient seedlings to supply the average pond, or two, will emerge in the spring, but often a quicker means of propagation is to divide a mature plant; for some plants this is the only means of propagation.

Descriptions of the best and, more to the point, the easiest ways to achieve satisfying results are given in the following Directory. You will also find information on the ideal planting depths for each species (how far below the surface of the water the top of the soil should be), and any particular likes and dislikes.

Acorus calamus
Sweet flag

True aquatic; Hardy herbaceous perennial

Natural habitat
Banks of rivers, streams and lakes

Ideal conditions
Shallow water, but will tolerate depths of around 15cm (6in) or more

Ideal planting depth
2.5–7.5cm (1–3in) below water

Light requirements
Enjoys full sun but is shade tolerant

Soil preference
Heavy clay or loam

Normal height
80–95cm (2½–3ft)

Flower type
Does not flower in the recognized sense; mature plants occasionally produce inflorescences

Flower colour
No flower; occasional pale buff inflorescence

Flowering time
Occasional inflorescence, early to midsummer

Propagation
By division of rhizome in early spring

Particulars
Acorus calamus originates from eastern Europe. It is believed to have been imported in early medieval times for use on flagstones, to mask unpleasant odours wafting up from the litter-strewn floors. Its sword-shaped, mid-green leaves sprout alternately from a creeping rhizome rootstock that is easily divided or trimmed back. Heights of 1m (3ft) or more are not uncommon, especially in ideal growing conditions and partial shade.

The leaves and rootstock of this plant exude a pleasant aroma when crushed – almost certainly why it was imported in the first place.

This plant can become rather large, so it is best suited to larger ponds and lakesides. If kept in smaller ponds, it will require regular trimming back to keep it under control.

Propagation is very easy: simply cut off the required length of rhizome and plant in wet conditions. This plant rarely, if ever, sets seed. Should it do so, the seeds will appear on an inflorescence in midsummer.

Little additional care is required as the plant is supplied with all the food it needs from the surrounding water.

Acorus calamus 'Variegatus'
Variegated sweet flag

True aquatic; Hardy herbaceous perennial

Natural habitat
Banks of rivers, streams and lakes

Ideal conditions
Shallow water, but will tolerate depths of 15cm (6in) or so

Ideal planting depth
2.5–7.5cm (1–3in) below water

Light requirements
Enjoys full sun but is shade tolerant

Soil preference
Heavy clay or loam

Normal height
80–95cm (2½–3ft)

Flower type
Does not flower in the recognized sense; mature plants occasionally produce inflorescences

Flower colour
No flower; occasional pale buff inflorescence. Grown for its variegated foliage rather than for its flowers

Flowering time
Occasional inflorescence, early to midsummer

Propagation
By division of rhizome in early spring

Particulars
Acorus calamus 'Variegatus' is grown principally for its very attractive, variegated foliage. Pink and cream shoots appear in early spring, sprouting alternately from a creeping rhizome rootstock that is easily divided and kept under control. More mature leaves lose their creamy appearance to become whiter with age. The vertical variegation on the leaves is almost a 50/50 split, with one half white and the other a soft mid-green. If they are crushed, the leaves and rootstock exude an aromatic fragrance. Heights of 90cm (3ft) or more are not uncommon, especially in ideal growing conditions and partial shade.

This plant is not as vigorous as the all-green variety so can be kept in a smaller pond, with the occasional trim back as necessary.

Propagation is very easy; merely cut off the length of rhizome that is required and plant in wet conditions. Little additional care, other than the occasional removal of leaves that are dying back, is required. The plant derives all the nutrients it requires from the surrounding water.

Acorus gramineus
Dwarf Japanese rush

Hardy evergreen perennial

Natural habitat
Moist areas

Ideal conditions
Moist (or place bottom of pot in water) in a sunny spot

Ideal planting depth
Just above the water surface, though will tolerate a depth of up to 5cm (2in)

Light requirements
Shade tolerant but enjoys full sun

Soil preference
Heavy loam, though tolerant of low peat content – up to 20% in wet conditions

Normal height
15–20cm (6–8in)

Flower type
Does not flower in the recognized sense; mature plants will occasionally produce inflorescences

Flower colour
No flower; occasional creamy buff inflorescence

Flowering time
Occasional inflorescence, early to midsummer

Propagation
By division of roots in spring

Particulars
A very attractive, low-growing plant, *Acorus gramineus* is very undemanding, and will grow happily for several years before requiring any attention or trimming back. Thick tufts of narrow leaves, with vertical stripes of green and white, sprout up from the multibranched, creeping roots at a steep angle. This gives a mature plant the appearance of a single tuft of leaf, with the relatively thin rhizome being completely hidden below the mass of foliage. The plant is evergreen in all but the harshest of conditions.

The plant's performance is enhanced with the addition of a little food in spring. This can be either a slow-release, granular fertilizer or a few small pellets of bone meal. Little extra care is required, apart from the removal of any dead or dying foliage, to maintain appearance as much as anything else. Any frost-damaged leaves should be trimmed back in early spring. Mature clumps should be divided every few years to maintain health and vigour.

Propagate by cutting off young pieces, preferably with some root on, and transferring them to another pot. Use a good heavy loam for the planting medium. The plant is relatively slow in making root, so take care not to disturb once it has been re-potted. It is best left in a shallow tray of water for at least six months before being moved to the pond environment.

Alisma parviflora
American water plantain

Hardy aquatic herbaceous perennial

Natural habitat
Muddy surrounds of ponds and lakes, in water up to 30cm (12in) deep

Ideal conditions
Shallow water

Ideal planting depth
0–15cm (0–6in) below water

Light requirements
Enjoys full sunlight but is shade tolerant

Soil preference
Heavy loam/clay variants as in natural habitats

Normal height
60–70cm (2–2½ft)

Flower type
Small, single flowers around 5mm (¼in) in diameter, clustered on tall, pyramidal panicles

Flower colour
Pale pink

Flowering time
Midsummer

Propagation
By seed collected in midsummer or division of crown in spring

Particulars
This wavy-edged water plantain's leaves are ovate and dark green with undulating edges and a bold rib effect along their length. Slender young leaves show through the water in late spring, when light levels are strong enough to trigger growth and the water has warmed a little. Once the leaves are well developed, in early summer, the plant will send up a flower panicle; mature plants have several. The small, three-petalled, pink flowers open steadily, from the bottom of the stem up, over two or three weeks. The stems themselves are pyramidal and multibranched. As the flowers die off they form seed heads. Flowering is usually over by midsummer. The foliage then dies back, forming an ugly mass of dying, dead and semi-decayed leaves. At this stage, preferably a little sooner, cut right back to just above soil level: this will encourage new leaves to form and prevent uncontrolled self-seeding – an event to be avoided in all but the largest lakes. Cutting back in this manner can trigger a second flowering before late autumn, though this depends upon where you live; the longer your summer, the greater your chances of a second flush. Before the onset of winter, remove all foliage to within 5cm (2in) of soil level to avoid needless detritus and pollution.

Collected seeds will germinate quite readily in water, taking two to six weeks. Plant out into moist conditions once large enough to handle and grow on until the following year, before planting out around the pond. Divide large plants in the spring by teasing apart the crowns that form around soil level, plant up in mesh baskets in a heavy clay or loam, and place in water.

Alisma plantago
Common water plantain

True aquatic; Hardy herbaceous perennial

Natural habitat
Muddy edges of ponds and lakes in water up to 30cm (12in) deep

Ideal conditions
Shallow water

Ideal planting depth
0–20cm (0–8in) below water

Light requirements
Enjoys full sunlight but is shade tolerant

Soil preference
Heavy loam and clay variants as in its natural habitat

Normal height
60–70cm (2–2½ft)

Flower type
Small, single flowers, approximately 5mm (¼in) in diameter, clustered on tall, pyramidal flowering panicles

Flower colour
Pale pink

Flowering time
Midsummer

Propagation
By seed in mid- to late summer or by division of crowns in spring

Particulars
Alisma plantago can be found in many natural wetland habitats, often growing in the shallows around lakes, ponds and slow-flowing streams and sometimes seen growing in the muddy areas above summer water levels.

The leaves are shaped a little like a stunted spear. They are light green and grow from the crown on pale green stems. They usually start to show through the water in mid-spring when the light levels are strong enough to trigger growth and the shallow water has warmed a little, however, they can appear earlier, or later, depending upon where you live. Once the leaves have become well developed, usually by late spring or early summer, the plant will send up a pyramidal flower spike; mature plants have several. The flowers open steadily over a two- or three-week period, forming seed heads as they die off. After flowering, and once the seeds are well formed, the foliage has the unfortunate habit of dying back. At this stage it is best to cut the plant right back to just above soil level. This will encourage new leaves to form and will also prevent the plant self-seeding everywhere – something you do not need in a small pond. Once ripe the seeds, as with all alismas, will drop into the water and float around for a while before sinking in amongst the rest of your plants to germinate the following year. Due to the readiness of deposited seed to germinate in wet or muddy conditions, *Alisma plantago* can take over if you do not exercise care.

If you are growing from seed, plant ripe seeds in shallow water and allow to germinate; this can take from two to six weeks. Leave these seedlings to grow until large enough to handle before pricking out into containers, then keep wet and grow on for the following season's use. To divide the root system, tease apart the multicrowned centre and plant up in heavy loam or clay before replacing in the pond.

Aponogeton distachyos
Water hawthorn/Cape pondweed

Deep water aquatic; Hardy perennial

Natural habitat
Ponds and lakes in water depths of 30–100cm (1–3ft)

Ideal conditions
Lightly shaded ponds in 45–60cm (1½–2ft) of water

Ideal planting depth
30–90cm (1–3ft) below water

Light requirements
Full sun to dappled shade

Soil preference
Heavy clay and loam

Normal height
Water surface level

Flower type
Elongated, orchid-like and heavily scented with an aroma similar to vanilla essence

Flower colour
White

Flowering time
Early spring to summer and late summer to the first frosts of winter

Propagation
By seed throughout the growing season or division of tubers in late spring

Particulars

The water hawthorn originated from the Cape area of South Africa, where the flowers are used as an ingredient in salads and the tubers are cooked for eating. It is often held to be one of the most desirable pond plants, flowering when your waterlilies are not, and with a very pleasant scent that carries long distances on late spring, early summer and autumn evenings. It rests in the height of summer, dying right back to soil level. Don't be concerned: as soon as the plant senses cooler conditions, it sends up new growth and flower buds. More plants have been thrown away because of this behaviour than I would like to count.

The heavily scented blooms appear amongst long, strap-like, bright green leaves that arrive soon after the frosts have finished. Leaves and flower buds often continue between frosts; the leaves can survive frosts but the flower buds do not. The flowers are uniquely shaped, being more akin to an orchid than anything else in the pond. The pure white, elliptical petals fork upwards and outwards from a single stem, with jet black anthers along their centres. The stems on both leaf and flower can become quite long under ideal conditions, reaching a metre (3ft) or more. The deeper the water, within its growing range, the larger the flower becomes, owing to the greater length of time it has to develop before surfacing.

A heavy feeder, it requires plenty of food to be at its best. At the very least it should have a biannual feed of several bone meal pellets. Without sufficient food it will produce fewer and smaller flowers. Little other care is needed.

These plants are readily pollinated by insects and produce a plentiful supply of seedlings that can become invasive. It is best to harvest the seedlings and grow them on elsewhere, in shallow water, to avoid any potential problems.

Baldellia ranunculoides
Lesser water plantain

True aquatic; Hardy herbaceous perennial

Natural habitat
Shallow margins of natural lakes and ponds

Ideal conditions
In very wet ground or, preferably, partially submerged

Ideal planting depth
0–5cm (0–2in) below water

Light requirements
Full sun

Soil preference
Heavy loam to clay

Normal height
10–15cm (4–6in)

Flower type
Single

Flower colour
Soft, pale pink

Flowering time
Early summer

Propagation
By seed in early spring

Particulars

This delightful plant is rarely on offer, which is a pity: it is ideal for the very small pond or water feature. It never gets very large, its dainty, spear-shaped, soft green foliage rarely extending beyond 10–15cm (4–6in) in length.

Being a true aquatic, it loves a slightly submerged situation in which it will always thrive. Leaves start to appear as soon as the water is warmed by late spring sunshine, reaching their full size over a period of about six weeks. Fine and delicate in appearance, the flower stems emerge in early summer to support whorls of small, pale pink, single flowers. These bloom in succession over two to three weeks, forming small globes of tiny seeds that, if not collected, will self-sow wherever they fall. Lesser water plantain requires little care apart from the removal of old foliage to prevent water pollution. It is very self-sufficient.

By far the best way to manage this plant is to collect the seeds as they ripen, from early to mid-spring: this will help to prevent over-abundance. Plant these seeds in shallow trays of wet soil and they will soon germinate, becoming large enough to plant out in late summer or the following spring.

Butomus umbellatus
Flowering rush/water gladiolus

True aquatic; Hardy herbaceous perennial

Natural habitat
Marshy areas alongside lakes and rivers

Ideal conditions
Soil level at or around water surface level

Ideal planting depth
5cm (2in) above water to 10cm (4in) below

Light requirements
Full sun

Soil preference
Heavy loam and clay

Normal height
90cm (3ft)

Flower type
Umbells of 30-plus single flowers on each flower head

Flower colour
Rose pink

Flowering time
Early to midsummer

Propagation
By division of tuberous root system in spring

Particulars
Butomus umbellatus is a must for any pond or water garden. A mature plant in full flower is a sight to behold. The triangular, somewhat sedge-like leaves have a purple tinge to them when they appear in late spring that is gradually lost as they grow and mature. Initially hard to see, the tall, cylindrical flower stems gradually appear from amongst this quite dense foliage, to flower from early to midsummer.

Flowering rush thrives in a clay-based medium with added food; peat-based mediums are best avoided. It will benefit from the addition of food soon after the new growth begins in spring or after division. This is best provided by pushing a few pellets of bone meal or a small amount of granular, slow-release fertilizer down into the root system. Being clump forming, it requires regular division to keep flowering at its best, as it can soon exhaust food supplies. Little other care is required apart from the removal of old foliage as and when needed.

The plant rarely sets seed in colder climes, requiring warmer, more certain conditions. In any case, growing from seed is a complex and frustrating experience and should be ignored for general purposes.

Masses of plants can be produced by annual division in spring. The plant, if provided with adequate food, will multiply readily, supplying plenty of propagation material. The root clumps are reminiscent of a rhizome but somewhat more bulb-like in behaviour. They can usually be teased apart using both hands. The use of a knife or spade will damage the plant, but may have to be resorted to for very large clumps. Plant divided clumps and place in very moist to wet conditions.

Calla palustris
Bog arum

True aquatic; Hardy herbaceous perennial

Natural habitat
Muddy or marshy ground around ponds and lakes

Ideal conditions
In the shallows around the margins of the pond with soil level at or around water level, though it will take up to 7.5cm (3in) of water cover

Ideal planting depth
5–7.5cm (2–3in) below water

Light requirements
Full sun

Soil preference
Heavy loam to clay; will tolerate some peat content

Normal height
15cm (6in)

Flower type
Arum-like spathe

Flower colour
Pure white

Flowering time
Midsummer

Propagation
By seed or division of horizontal stem in late spring

Particulars

Calla palustris, the bog arum, is ideal for concealing the unsightly edges of man-made ponds. It meanders around the edges, sometimes spreading out into the pool, and masks all beneath it. It is a hardy plant, succumbing to winter only in the harshest of conditions.

Its glossy green, heart-shaped leaves are supported on short stems that shoot up from a soft, delicate, rhizome-like and often multibranched, bright green creeping stem. The bright white arum-like flowers appear along the length of this stem in midsummer, lighting up the pond. Any leaves that die back should be removed to encourage new growth.

Calla palustris shows significant increases in size and vigour if fed well in early summer. Although the plant feeds well from the water it is in, I would advise providing additional food, in the form of bone meal or slow-release fertilizer, for best results in the average pond.

As for general care, little is needed other than the removal of old leafy growth, which benefits the plant, and helps to maintain its appearance. It keeps the plant open and free from fungal problems and avoids the pollution that slowly rotting vegetation can cause. Pinching out the pointed growing tip will encourage more branching growth and give the plant a fuller look.

The flowers are pollinated by a multitude of insects and produce viable seed, but this can be very difficult to germinate, and may take months or years. By far the best method of propagation is simple stem division. Remove sections of stem about 10cm (4in) long and plant them up in a sunny spot, in wet conditions.

Caltha palustris
Marsh marigold

True aquatic; Hardy herbaceous perennial

Natural habitat
Muddy and marshy ground around ponds, rivers, lakes and streams, and on stream and river banks

Ideal conditions
In the shallows around the margins of the pond; will quite happily take up to 7.5cm (3in) of water over the crown, once it is established

Ideal planting depth
2–7.5cm (¾–3in) below water

Light requirements
Full sun to dappled shade

Soil preference
Heavy loam to clay

Normal height
25–30cm (10–12in)

Flower type
Single

Flower colour
Golden yellow

Flowering time
Spring

Propagation
By seed in early winter or division of crown in late summer

Particulars
Caltha palustris, commonly known as marsh marigold, is one of the first plants to flower in early spring. It brings life and colour to what would otherwise be a fairly dull pond at that time of year.

A mature plant can bear as many as 50 blooms in succession, lasting over several weeks, and a plant can often be made to flower again in the autumn by removing all growth after the first flowering has finished in late spring. It is always worth a try.

Bright green leaves start to appear in late winter and form a dense clump of orbicular, mid-green leaves by early spring. The branched flower stems appear amongst this foliage around the same time, soon to flower in profusion.

This plant will grow in shade quite happily, but has a tendency to be somewhat straggly under these conditions – it grows at its best in maximum light. It also has a tendency to develop a mild mildew over the stems. This is nothing to be concerned about, as it is endemic to the plant; just remove any affected leaves and stems as it manifests. Being fairly self-sufficient it requires little care other than the removal of old growth as it dies back. It draws all the nutrients it requires from the surrounding water; you can add extra food in late autumn if you wish, but this is rarely necessary.

Caltha palustris sets seed quite readily. The best results are obtained by allowing them to germinate where they fall, then harvesting the young plants the following spring. The roots of mature plants can be divided every two or three years, and the resultant small plants planted up in a heavy loam medium in moist conditions; they should not be allowed to dry out.

Caltha palustris var. *alba*
White marsh marigold

Hardy herbaceous perennial

Natural habitat
Marshy areas and wetlands, stream and river banks

Ideal conditions
Muddy ground around the margins of the pond or with the soil level of the pot just above water level

Ideal planting depth
2–7.5cm (¾–3in) above water to 2.5cm (1in) below

Light requirements
Full sun to dappled shade

Soil preference
Heavy loam to clay

Normal height
15–25cm (6–10in)

Flower type
Single

Flower colour
Creamy white tinged with pink at the centre

Flowering time
Late winter to early spring

Propagation
By seed in early winter or division of crown in late summer

Particulars
Caltha palustris var. *alba* is a native of the Himalayas and at its best in maximum light conditions. It is one of the first plants to flower in early spring, with the buds appearing in late winter, forming a creamy white clump well before the foliage opens out. Like all calthas, it brings life and colour to what would otherwise be a fairly dull pond. A mature plant can bear as many as 50 blooms in succession, lasting over several weeks.

The bright green, heart-shaped leaves, with their indented edges, start to appear in late winter and form a dense clump by mid-spring.

The care required is fairly minimal. A little extra food in late autumn certainly makes a difference to the number of flowers produced the following spring, as does the removal of old leaves as they die back throughout the season.

This marsh marigold sets seed somewhat sparingly. To obtain the best results from seeds, allow them to germinate where they fall and harvest the young plants the following spring.

The roots of mature plants can be divided every two or three years, and the resultant small plants planted up in a heavy loam medium in moist conditions; they should not be allowed to dry out.

Caltha plena 'Multiplex'

Double marsh marigold

True aquatic; Hardy herbaceous perennial

Natural habitat
Marshy areas and wetlands, stream and river banks

Ideal conditions
In muddy ground around the margins of a pond, or shallow water

Ideal planting depth
5cm (2in) above water to 2.5cm (1in) below

Light requirements
Full sun to dappled shade

Soil preference
Heavy loam to clay

Normal height
25–30cm (10–12in)

Flower type
Very double

Flower colour
Deep golden yellow

Flowering time
Late spring

Propagation
By division of crown from late summer to early autumn

Particulars
Caltha plena, often labelled *Caltha* 'Multiplex', is the most showy plant of the genus; flowering a couple of weeks later than *Caltha palustris*, its dome of massed, deep golden flowers is not to be missed.

The soft, mid-green, orbicular leaves of this plant are sometimes confused with that of *Caltha palustris* var. *alba* as they have similar indentations around the edges of the leaves. However, *Caltha plena* flowers later and its foliage appears before the flowers form. Several of its almost perfect half-ball flower domes will appear together on one branched stem.

The plant enjoys a wet to shallow water situation, ideally with the water just over the top of the pot or soil. If you feed this plant with bone meal or slow-release fertilizer in late autumn, it will reward you by producing more flowers the following spring. Other than this, little care is required apart from the removal of old growth as it dies back.

It can only be propagated by division, as it does not set seed. The root mass is easy to pull apart – easing the multiple crowns apart without damaging them is the trick. A mature plant may well produce four or five plants each year, and should be divided every three years or so, to maintain its health and vigour. Plant divided plants in either a good heavy loam or a clay-based, loamy medium with a little bone meal and place in moist to wet conditions.

Caltha polypetala
Giant marsh marigold

Hardy herbaceous perennial

Natural habitat
Marshy areas and wetlands, stream and river banks

Ideal conditions
Muddy and marshy ground around ponds, in shallow water of up to 10cm (4in)

Ideal planting depth
Up to 10cm (4in) below water

Light requirements
Full sun to dappled shade

Soil preference
Heavy loam and clay

Normal height
Up to 60cm (2ft)

Flower type
Large, single

Flower colour
Deep golden yellow

Flowering time
Late spring

Propagation
Best done by seed in early winter or by viviparous stems which root naturally from late spring to midsummer

Particulars
Caltha polypetala is not as showy as other calthas, having fewer blooms than most, but what it lacks in quantity it makes up for in size. The flowers, appearing in late spring, can be 5cm (2in) or more across. Its very large leaves are the earliest to appear of all the calthas, often to be seen not long after midwinter.

Being a very large plant, it is best suited to the larger planting scheme. It is not ideal for the small garden pond: its drooping stems have a habit of reaching down to the mud and rooting up so it can be very invasive, and if left to its own devices will often take over.

This plant derives all the nutrients it requires from the surrounding water; extra food is not needed. The care required is quite minimal, removal of old leaves and excessive growth being all that is necessary.

Its natural, self-propagating habit makes it very easy to cultivate more plants, and it does produce viable seed if this is needed. Grow from seed in the same way as for *Caltha palustris* (see p 41).

Carex elata 'Aurea'
Bowles' golden sedge

True aquatic; Hardy herbaceous perennial

Natural habitat
Marshy banks of lakes and rivers

Ideal conditions
Planted with the water level to the top of the soil

Ideal planting depth
0–5cm (0–2in) below water

Light requirements
Full sun to dappled shade

Soil preference
Heavy loam

Normal height
60cm (2ft)

Flower type
No significant flower: seed spikelet

Flower colour
No significant flower; brown seed head

Flowering time
Seed heads in early summer

Propagation
By division of root mass in spring

Particulars
Bowles' golden sedge, as it is commonly known in the aquatic world, is a strikingly beautiful and showy plant that will grace any pond. The long, slender golden leaves, sometimes very lightly edged with green, arch gently outwards from a dense, clump-forming root mass. Although the plant will eventually form a dense and quite large clump, this takes several years and it is not particularly invasive. It doesn't have a flower as such, more a show of fluffy pollen on a nascent brown seed head borne at the tip of a long slender stem.

Once planted up this cultivar requires little care other than the removal of old growth before the appearance of new growth in the spring. Add a little food, in the form of bone meal, when re-potting. After this, the plant will draw all that it requires from the surrounding water.

The seed, although fertile, does not always produce golden-leaved plants; a high percentage revert to plain green. For this reason it is best propagated by carefully dividing the root mass in early spring, as soon as the new growth appears. Re-pot the plant using heavy soil with little or no peat content.

Carex pendula
Weeping sedge/pendulous sedge

Hardy evergreen perennial

Natural habitat
Banks of lakes, rivers and ponds, marshy and damp ground

Ideal conditions
Marshy ground

Ideal planting depth
5cm (2in) above water to water level

Light requirements
Dappled shade or full sun

Soil preference
Heavy loam and clay; will tolerate some peat content

Normal height
Up to 1.5m (5ft)

Flower type
No noticeable flower, but pendulous, catkin-like seed heads

Flower colour
No noticeable flower; light brown seed heads

Flowering time
Seed heads from early to midsummer

Propagation
By seed or by division of crown in spring

Particulars
Carex pendula forms very large, spectacular stately clumps quite rapidly. It is a plant best suited to the larger pond or lake. Control can be exercised to some extent by planting in a solid plastic pot rather than the usual mesh basket. If planted in open ground it can become very large indeed, with the gently arching leaves forming a clump well over a metre (3ft) in diameter.

In late spring, tall flower (seed head) stems emerge from amongst these masses of narrow, mid-green leaves. The flower itself is barely noticeable; more a showing of pollen and a soft brown downy material than anything else.

The light brown seed heads form gradually over a period of several weeks, emerging from the almost feathery down to ripen in late summer. Seed heads should be removed before they ripen, to avoid an over-population due to self-seeding.

Little general care is required. As the plant derives all it needs from the water and soil it is planted in, additional feeding is rarely necessary. Little benefit is derived from the removal of old leaves, except for appearance' sake, and this task, being a somewhat fiddly one, is usually only carried out by the very dedicated.

By far the easiest method of propagation is to divide large root clumps in the spring – many plants can be obtained from one mature plant. Collect seed in the late summer and plant it in moist conditions, in a loam-based medium, early the following spring. Germination of the seeds usually takes around two weeks.

Carex pseudocyperus
Sedge grass

Hardy herbaceous perennial

Natural habitat
Banks of lakes, rivers and streams

Ideal conditions
Very moist to wet areas bordering natural bodies of water

Ideal planting depth
2.5cm (1in) above water to 5cm (2in) below

Light requirements
Partial to full sun

Soil preference
Heavy soil to clay

Normal height
60cm (2ft)

Flower type
No significant flower; pendulous, grain-like seed head

Flower colour
Show of pollen on seed spikelet

Flowering time
Seed heads in early summer

Propagation
By seed in late summer or division of multi-head crown in spring

Particulars
This species has a distinctive and attractive seed head, somewhat reminiscent of a wheat ear. It is particularly attractive in early summer when the new, light green seed heads have formed and dance in the breeze. The slender foliage, light to mid-green, has a fairly erect growth pattern, arching outwards only towards the top third of the plant, after reaching full size. *Carex pseudocyperus* is clump forming and inclined to be quite vigorous under ideal conditions. In temperate climes it can retain leaves through the year, almost deserving evergreen status. The seed heads appear in early summer, after a brief flowering period. They are held at intervals by fine stalks, dangling pendulously, along the upper third of each of the long, slender, light brown stems.

This plant is quite happy in most situations, from being almost submerged to being planted in moist ground, but the wetter it is, the more vigorous it tends to be. Little extra care is needed as this plant is self-sufficient, being able to draw all the nutrients it requires from the surrounding water. The removal of old leaves maintains the aesthetic appeal of the plant, but is not necessary for any other reason. A good trim in late winter, as soon as the frosts abate, is by far the best way of keeping a tidy plant.

Propagation is by seed in late summer, planting in moist conditions, or by root division in spring. It is advisable to remove the seed heads before they ripen, turning brown as they do so, to prevent overpopulation: the plant self-seeds very successfully. The root system on a mature plant (three years plus) is extremely dense and best divided using a spade or two forks to reduce wear and tear on the thumbs!

Carex riparia
Water sedge/greater pond sedge

Hardy evergreen perennial

Natural habitat
Banks of rivers, lakes and ponds, from moist ground to partial submergence

Ideal conditions
Shallow water to marshy ground

Ideal planting depth
2.5cm (1in) above water to 5cm (2in) below

Light requirements
Full sun to dappled shade

Soil preference
Heavy loam to clay

Normal height
Up to 1m (3ft)

Flower type
No significant flower; black seed heads

Flower colour
No significant flower; show of pollen on pre-pubescent seed head

Flowering time
Seed heads in midsummer

Propagation
Best carried out by division of roots as seed can be extremely difficult and erratic, on occasion taking several years to germinate even in ideal conditions

Particulars
Carex riparia has long, slender, blue-green leaves that, under ideal conditions, can reach 1m (3ft). The plant retains its leaves under all but the harshest of conditions, bringing it into the evergreen category.

It is extremely vigorous, spreading rapidly via runners, making it ideal for stabilizing the banks of lakes and rivers. It bears striking, dark brown to black seed heads in midsummer, rising up out amongst the dense foliage.

If *Carex riparia* is used in a small pond, it is best kept in a solid pot in order to control its vigorous habit: left to its own devices, this plant will colonize your pond. However, it is attractive and evergreen, making it very worthwhile if kept under tight control.

Little care is required other than trimming back old foliage after winter has passed. The plant is very self-sufficient, drawing all the nutrients it needs from the pond.

Propagation is best carried out by root division; use a spade to cut the clump up or two very strong forks to prise it apart. Hands are useless as the root mass is very dense and tough.

Propagation by seed is difficult as the seed often requires several winters before it will germinate, but it is always worth a try, even if just for fun. Plant in a moist tray, cover very lightly with soil or vermiculite, and keep moist at all times until the seedlings are ready for pricking out.

Cotula coronopifolia
Golden buttons/brass buttons

Half-hardy annual

Natural habitat
Marshy or moist ground

Ideal conditions
Marshy ground as underplanting to tall plants

Ideal planting depth
0–5cm (0–2in) below water

Light requirements
Full sun

Soil preference
Heavy loam with a little peat content

Normal height
15–20cm (6–8in)

Flower type
Button-head with close-knit petals

Flower colour
Light golden yellow

Flowering time
All summer

Propagation
By seed in spring, or stem cuttings from late spring to early summer

Particulars

Cotula coronopifolia is a lovely plant, ideally suited to hiding the edges of ponds and bare soil in containers. Once summer arrives, the plant will almost constantly be covered with masses of golden, button-like flowers, borne upwards from densely branched, light green foliage. It self-seeds very readily into moist ground and this habit, combined with its easily rooted, low-growing stems, make it a plant that does require some control.

For the greatest impact it is best to remove the old flowers as soon as they start to brown. As this is the seed development stage, removal will also help to control the spread of the plant; if left to its own devices, it will colonize a fairly large area quite rapidly.

Cotula coronopifolia is great for low-growing summer colour. Just one plant planted in late spring will make a considerable clump well before winter sets in. Although regarded as a hardy perennial by some, it is best to treat it as an annual as it often succumbs to harsh winters, even in temperate zones.

Caring for this plant is extremely easy; remove old flowers and excess foliage to control self-seeding and pull off any foliage that has died due to frosting to avoid unwanted pollution: rotting vegetation could end up in the pond, giving an oily sheen to the water, and forming noxious gasses. The plant will draw all the food it requires from its surroundings; no additional food should be provided – unless you want a jungle.

Propagation is simplicity itself; allow it to self-seed and move the new plants where you will as soon as they are large enough. Seeds can be stored and planted in situ – in moist ground, in early spring – to produce the new season's flowers.

Cyperus involucratus
Umbrella grass

Half-hardy herbaceous perennial

Natural habitat
Marshy areas, banks of natural lakes and ponds

Ideal conditions
Very moist to wet ground

Ideal planting depth
0–5cm (0–2in) below water

Light requirements
Full sun to partial shade

Soil preference
Heavy loam

Normal height
60cm (2ft) plus

Flower type
No significant flower; attractive seed heads with clusters of seeds arranged on slender stems

Flower colour
No significant flower; pale green seeds

Flowering time
Seed heads in early summer

Propagation
By seed or division of roots in spring

Particulars
This plant is also known as *Cyperus flabelliformis, C. glaber* and *C. alternifolius* hort. (cultivated garden form). Its lush, slender, fresh green and gently arching leaves form dense clumps in early summer.

The plant's main feature is its very decorative umbrella-like heads which have fascinating whorls, or clusters, of spiky seeds. These are supported on thin stems that arch out from the tip of the main supporting stem. Both seeds and foliage turn a light brown in autumn. The species is quite vigorous and will form large clumps in the space of two seasons. Control can be exercised by planting in a solid pot rather than a mesh planting basket: this will contain and restrict root expansion.

Trimming back the old foliage is best left until spring, as it does provide some frost protection and can be quite attractive through the winter, providing a decorative effect. However, the plant can be a little tender in harsh climes, and additional protection may be required, particularly if it is subjected to severe frosts.

Cyperus involucratus is extremely easy to grow from seed. Harvest them before they scatter and sow in late spring, in moist soil. Leave the seeds standing in a tray of shallow water, ensuring that it remains moist at all times. There is no need to cover. Germination takes two to three weeks, and the seedlings will be ready for pricking out around three weeks after that. The root mass is so dense it is best divided with a spade, in early spring, and cut to size. Once growth starts the plant will soon regenerate and rapidly fill its container.

Cyperus longus
Sweet galingale/galingale

Hardy herbaceous perennial

Natural habitat
Surrounds of natural lakes and ponds

Ideal conditions
Moist to very wet ground

Ideal planting depth
5cm (2in) above to 20cm (8in) below water

Light requirements
Full sun to partial shade

Soil preference
Heavy loam

Normal height
1.2–1.5m (4–5ft)

Flower type
Grassy spikelets

Flower colour
Brown

Flowering time
Midsummer

Propagation
By division of roots in early spring

Particulars
This is a showy and attractive plant that should not be missed. Definitely belonging under the 'architectural' classification used by many nurseries, it really is magnificent.

Sweet galingale is very vigorous and will rapidly colonize large areas if given half the chance, but this vigour can be contained with the use of a solid pot. It is also very adaptable, growing in anything from moist to submerged conditions and even in containers if they are kept permanently moist. The common name refers to its herbal attributes – it was used, ground up, in medieval cooking.

The long, arching, mid-green leaves have a lightly serrated edge, similar to pampas grass, and can inflict tiny cuts if handled by the unwary. The lush foliage mass is quite dense, making it difficult to see the triangular flower stems until they start to open and show off their umbels of grass-like, light brown spikelets. The foliage will last well into early winter, when it should be trimmed back to avoid dead leaves polluting the pond. New growth is slow to appear, usually in late spring, but once started it grows rapidly.

Propagation of this plant is best carried out by root division, using a sharp spade or two strong forks as the root system is very dense and tough. Growing from seed is somewhat complex and best left alone. For all normal purposes more than enough material can be obtained from the root system, which produces many young growing shoots.

Cyperus rotundus
(No common name)

Hardy herbaceous perennial

Natural habitat
Marshy and damp conditions

Ideal conditions
In water up to soil level

Ideal planting depth
0–5cm (0–2in) below water

Light requirements
Full sun

Soil preference
Not fussy, providing peat content does not exceed 20%

Normal height
80–90cm (2½–3ft)

Flower type
No significant flower; grass-like globular seed head

Flower colour
No significant flower; brown seed head

Flowering time
Seed heads in midsummer

Propagation
By division of roots in early winter

Particulars

Another species that will definitely fall under the 'architectural' classification used by many nurseries, this very striking and attractive plant is rarely seen and is not usually available in aquatic centres. It should be. The globe-like seed heads, mid- to dark brown, are borne in clusters of three. They consist of many tiny, individual seed pods of feather-like construction and appear in midsummer at the top of tall, triangular stems, along with three leaf-like extensions, giving an almost umbrella-like appearance. The long, narrow mid- to dark green leaves arch upwards and outwards from a clump-forming root mass that will reach a good size in just a few seasons.

Cyperus rotundus does appreciate a little extra food in spring. This makes the resultant foliage almost shine with vigour when it appears in late spring/early summer. Just like *C. longus*, it is a late starter, but once it does get going it grows rapidly, reaching full size in just a few weeks. All old leaves should be removed as they die off to avoid unnecessary pollution, especially just prior to winter, when leaf fall is at its greatest. It is not an invasive plant but can get rather large if left for too long without some control. The best methods of control are regular trimming of roots or planting in a solid pot.

Propagation is best carried out by root division; prise apart the dense root system of a mature plant and plant in a good loam-based compost. A sharp knife may well be necessary as the root system is very tough and somewhat wiry. Growing from seed is more than a little difficult, and yields mixed results; it is not worth bothering with for normal purposes. Being so attractive it is very sought after, by those who know of its existence, so any spare plants you produce will be easy to dispose of.

Equisetum japonicum
Horsetail

Hardy herbaceous perennial

Natural habitat
Marshy ground

Ideal conditions
Moist with plenty of humus

Ideal planting depth
*5cm (2in) above to 2.5cm (1in)
below water*

Light requirements
Full sun to partial shade

Soil preference
Loam with some peat content

Normal height
45cm (1½ft)

Flower type
*Does not flower in the recognized sense;
produces inflorescences*

Flower colour
*No significant flower; brown spores contained
in tight, bud-like inflorescences*

Flowering time
*No significant flower; produces spores
in late summer*

Propagation
By division of roots in spring

Particulars
This unusual plant, with its cylindrical leaves,
is one of the oldest species on earth; a tough,
but attractive survivor. The leaves are more
akin to stems, being round, slender and with
light brown bands at each node along their
whole length.

The plant extends itself via a wiry, creeping
rootstock that is well supplied with
emergent buds. Once established it can
spread fairly rapidly, so care should be taken
to ensure it does not invade areas where it
is not wanted.

Although it can remain evergreen in gentle
climes, it is best regarded as a perennial.
Equisetum japonicum requires only basic care;
the occasional removal of old foliage will aid
its overall health and vigour. In spring a little
extra food, in the form of bone meal, is
always appreciated.

Propagation is simplicity itself; remove any
spare roots from around the pot or container
in spring, plant in a fresh pot about 2.5cm
(1in) below soil level, keep moist, and new
growth will soon appear.

If you need to divide roots, cut up clumps
with a knife, re-pot and keep moist.

Eriophorum angustifolium
Cotton grass

Hardy evergreen

Natural habitat
Peat bogs and acidic ground

Ideal conditions
Boggy, marshy ground with plenty of peat; shallow water

Ideal planting depth
0–10cm (0–4in) below water

Light requirements
Full sun

Soil preference
Acidic

Normal height
30cm (12in)

Flower type
Like cotton wool in appearance

Flower colour
White

Flowering time
Summer

Propagation
By division of roots in spring or from seed in late spring

Particulars
Cotton grass produces a regular supply of stiff, tough, rush-like leaves from loosely amalgamated clumps. It is normally found in boggy areas so has evolved naturally to enjoy acidic, peaty conditions – a break from the norm you might say. Most marginals and aquatics evolved in water-retentive, heavy loam, but this plant, although it will grow in such soil, does not thrive in it.

The leaf colour varies from reddish brown to olive green, the mix depending upon each individual situation; exposure and temperature seem to be the controlling factors. The leaves may well start out olive green and turn colour in autumn, or stay green throughout the season.

The plant itself is a real survivor with a strong determination to spread. This it does via a tough, woody rhizome; it can colonize considerable areas in just two or three seasons. Control can be exercised through regular trimming of the root system or by planting in a solid pot.

General care amounts to the removal of old foliage, control of the root system and extra food in spring – a little bone meal is sufficient.

Propagate by harvesting the ever-ready rootstock or by harvesting seed before it blows away on the ripened, woolly white fluff. Plant in moist ground straight away and before too long your new plants will appear.

Geum rivale
Water avens

Hardy herbaceous perennial

Natural habitat
Stream and river banks

Ideal conditions
Marshy, moist ground

Ideal planting depth
5cm (2in) above to 2.5cm (1in) below water

Light requirements
Full sun to dappled shade

Soil preference
Heavy loam with a little humus

Normal height
30cm (12in)

Flower type
Pendulous bell, single

Flower colour
Orange/light brown

Flowering time
Early summer

Propagation
By seed or division of roots from mid- to late spring

Particulars
Water avens is vastly underrated. It is a plant that should be seen more often. Its compact, deeply lobed, green leaves are soft to the touch, and the plant forms dense clumps, slowly colonizing areas of river banks.

Lovely small, orange-brown, bell-like flowers appear in early summer rising above the foliage on stems, to nod in the breeze. The flowers eventually give way to furry, mace-like seed heads that are attractive in their own right.

Water avens is easy to care for, being more or less self-sufficient, but nevertheless enjoying a little extra food, in the form of bone meal, in early spring. Old foliage should be removed after it has died back for appearance' sake.

Propagation by seed is straightforward; plant in damp soil, cover lightly, place in a warm, shady spot and let nature take its course. Mature clumps should be divided every three years or so to maintain the health of the plant. **55**

Glyceria aquatica variegata
Striped water grass

True aquatic; Hardy herbaceous perennial

Natural habitat
Margins of natural bodies of water

Ideal conditions
Shallow water

Ideal planting depth
0–30cm (0–12in) below water

Light requirements
Full sun but will tolerate dappled shade

Soil preference
Heavy loam to clay

Normal height
Up to 1m (3ft)

Flower type
Grass-like, fluffy

Flower colour
Pale buff

Flowering time
Mid- to late summer

Propagation
By division of roots, from spring through to the end of summer

Particulars
This true aquatic has bold leaves with vertical stripes of green and creamy-white. Young growth is often tinged and flushed with pink, but this is lost as it matures.

Striped water grass is not a choice for the faint-hearted, being suitable only for the larger plantings required around big ponds and lakes. The plant possesses a vigorous, invasive root system that spreads rapidly throughout the growing season, and is quite capable of taking over a small garden pond if given full reign, smothering other, less able plants. Nevertheless, it is attractive and if you are prepared to maintain control – by trimming the root system regularly – it is well worthwhile. The root mass is very dense so you will need a sharp knife to trim it – take care not to cut the pond liner as well. The bulk of the growth should be removed before winter, as should any old and decaying leaves, in order to avoid pollution from rotting vegetation. There is no need for any additional food.

To propagate, merely re-pot the well-rooted excess from root trimmings and submerge. This can be done from spring right through to the end of summer.

Gratiola officinalis
Water hyssop

Hardy herbaceous perennial

Natural habitat
Shallow margins and banks of lakes, rivers and streams

Ideal conditions
Shallow water

Ideal planting depth
0–2.5cm (0–1in) below water

Light requirements
Full sun

Soil preference
Mid- to heavy loam and clay

Normal height
45cm (1½ft)

Flower type
Single, multiflorus

Flower colour
White

Flowering time
Summer

Propagation
By seed, cuttings or division of roots from mid- to late spring

Particulars
Another plant that should be seen more often. White-flowered plants make a pleasant change from the yellows that predominate around most ponds.

Erect, red-tinged stems support light green, elliptic leaves along their whole length. The delicate white flowers appear in succession, from the bottom up, borne on little stems that sprout from the leaf node.

Water hyssop is clump forming but not in an invasive way: it is easily divided and cared for. Stems should be allowed to die back in winter and removed in early spring, before new growth commences. This affords frost protection – the plant can be a little tender under harsh conditions.

Taking tip cuttings in late spring is perhaps the easiest way to propagate this plant. Just remove the top 5cm (2in) of the stem, plant in a pot of moist soil and place in a sheltered area; mother nature will do the rest, providing you with a new plant in two to three weeks.

To divide the roots of mature clumps, use your thumbs to tease them apart. Sow fresh seed in moist soil or compost, cover lightly, and place in a warm area. Prick out when the seedlings are about 5cm (2in) tall.

Hippuris vulgaris
Water horsetail

True aquatic; Hardy herbaceous perennial

Natural habitat
The shallow margins of natural lakes and ponds

Ideal conditions
Shallow water

Ideal planting depth
0–5cm (0–2in) below water

Light requirements
Full sun to partial shade

Soil preference
Heavy loam to clay

Normal height
Up to 30cm (12in)

Flower type
No significant flower

Flower colour
No significant flower

Flowering time
No significant flower

Propagation
By division of roots from mid- to late spring

Particulars
Another true aquatic plant that just loves shallow water. It is grown in the main for the unusual foliage it produces. This appears almost like a small forest, spreading via a sprawling, invasive root system. Though often sold as an oxygenating plant, its underwater foliage tends to die off quite rapidly and become sparse, so it provides little benefit as far as oxygenation is concerned. *Hippuris vulgaris'* main contribution is its rapid consumption of nitrates. These it converts into foliage at an impressive rate, thereby helping to maintain a clear pond.

With its invasive root system, it is a plant that requires control. This can be maintained by regular trimming of the root system or containing in a solid pot. Remove as much of the old foliage as possible, on a regular basis, to prevent unnecessary pollution.

Propagation, if it is ever needed, is by root division. Utilize some of the trimmings; plant in fresh soil, and partly submerge.

Hottonia palustris
Water violet

True aquatic; Hardy evergreen perennial

Natural habitat
Wetlands

Ideal conditions
Shallow water margins of natural lakes and ponds

Ideal planting depth
2.5–45cm (1–18in) below water

Light requirements
Full sun

Soil preference
Heavy loam to clay

Normal height
15cm (6in) above water if grown as a marginal

Flower type
Single

Flower colour
Pale violet to white

Flowering time
Midsummer

Propagation
By root-bearing stem cuttings

Particulars
This plant is another true aquatic and will grow in water up to 45cm (18in) deep quite happily. It does the work of a true oxygenator, bearing life-giving, oxygenating leaves along the whole length of its stem. It is not as invasive as many oxygenators sold in bunch form and is far more attractive and adaptable than most. Definitely not a plant to be missed, whether as an oxygenator or a marginal.

Grown as a marginal, this can be a very attractive plant indeed. Its light green, elliptic, deeply serrated leaves are borne on erect stems, well above the water, giving an almost feathery appearance. They form dense clumps at the water's edge, even scrambling over the edge into moist ground where they are also quite happy. In the summer months, lovely little violet flowers appear from amongst the foliage to provide a delightful show. The number of flowers really depends upon the size of plant: the more mature the plant, the greater the number of flowers produced.

The care required is minimal, removal of old foliage being the main requirement. The plant has no need for additional food, deriving all it requires from the surrounding water.

Propagation is relatively simple; take stem cuttings approximately 7.5cm (3in) long and plant them in heavy soil, under water. Growing them out of water brings a high failure rate; for normal purposes it is not worth bothering with.

Houttuynia cordata and cultivars ('Plena' shown below)
Orange peel plant

Hardy herbaceous perennial

Natural habitat
Moist ground

Ideal conditions
Any damp to wet ground

Ideal planting depth
7.5cm (3in) above to soil at water

Light requirements
Full sun to partial shade

Soil preference
Most soils that are not too acidic

Flower type
Single or double, depending upon the cultivar

Flower colour
White

Flowering time
Early to midsummer

Normal height
Up to 30cm (12in)

Propagation
By division of roots from mid- to late spring

Particulars
Houttuynia cordata cultivars have crossed over from use in herbaceous perennial borders to use in marginal situations. Aquatic growers, looking to expand the range of plants on offer, noticed that *Houttuynia cordata* thrived in the moist conditions surrounding ponds and even adapted to growing in water.

If the foliage, stems or roots are crushed, they exude a strong scent of orange peel. From early summer right up until the frosts begin, attractive blue-green, heart-shaped leaves are borne on erect stems that are tinged with red There are two forms of this plain-leaved variety; *Houttuynia cordata* has single flowers and *H. c.* 'Flore Pleno' double. Do try to obtain the double variety as the flower is well worth it; snow white and nestling amongst the blue-green foliage, they make for a very attractive addition to the pond.

The plant can be vigorous and invasive; control of the root system should be exercised or it will colonize large areas. A little extra food in spring, in the form of bone meal, will not go amiss – you will be rewarded with even more foliage.

Propagation is by root cuttings, carried out simply by trimming back the root system and planting the cuttings.

Houttuynia cordata 'Chameleon'
Variegated orange peel plant/chameleon plant

Hardy herbaceous perennial

Natural habitat
Moist ground

Ideal conditions
Any damp to wet ground

Ideal planting depth
7.5cm (3in) above to soil at water level

Light requirements
Full sun to partial shade

Soil preference
Most soils that are not too acidic

Normal height
Up to 30cm (12in)

Flower type
Single

Flower colour
White

Flowering time
Early to midsummer

Propagation
By division of roots from mid- to late spring

Particulars

In the same way as other *Houttuynia cordata* cultivars, 'Chameleon' has crossed over from use in herbaceous perennial borders, and if its foliage, stems or roots are crushed, they exude a strong scent of orange peel.

The very attractive leaves are heart-shaped and heavily mottled with shades of cream, green, yellow and red. They are borne on erect stems that are also tinged with red, from early summer right up until the frosts begin. This plant is grown for its beautiful foliage; the single white flower pales in comparison, barely noticeable in the riot of colour the leaves provide.

The plant can be vigorous and invasive; control of the root system should be exercised or it will colonize large areas. A little extra food, such as bone meal, can be added in spring – the reward of extra, and more vivid foliage is well worth the effort.

Propagation is by root cuttings, carried out simply by trimming back the root system, from mid- to late spring, and planting the cuttings.

Iris ensata cultivars ('Miyako-oki' shown below)
Japanese flag/clematis-flowered iris

Hardy herbaceous perennial

Natural habitat
Moist ground, drying out in winter

Ideal conditions
Wet ground in summer, drier in winter

Ideal planting depth
5cm (2in) above to soil at water level

Light requirements
Full sun to partial shade

Soil preference
Medium loam with plenty of humus and nutrients

Normal height
Up to 90cm (3ft)

Flower type
Large-petalled with varying forms, depending upon the cultivar

Flower colour
Variable and numerous, depending upon the cultivar

Flowering time
Early to midsummer

Propagation
By division of roots in spring or early autumn

Particulars

The cultivars of *Iris ensata* are truly magnificent plants. Their very showy flowers take many different forms, from narrow petals to broad, from pure white to deep purple – the range is extensive to say the least. *Iris ensata* cvs can be real show-offs, especially if you have the larger-bloomed varieties, but they are not over-vigorous, so there is little fear of them taking over. They should not be missed.

These plants are not true aquatics; while they enjoy a wet situation in the summer months, they will suffer, and even die, if left in water all year round. They do need to dry out to some extent in the winter, in a fairly frost-free area. For best results, remove the plant from the water in late summer, dig a hole in a spare corner of your garden and sink the plant in, pot and all. Leave it there until late spring, when it will enjoy going back into the water, just as its new growth is starting.

Old leaves should be left in place, to prevent ingress of water, and removed in early spring, before new growth appears. If the leaves are removed before winter, water that collects in the exposed hollow tubes may freeze, breaking the cell walls of the plant and thus killing it. The plant requires the addition of extra food every spring, or weak foliage and flowers will result.

Propagation is best done by dividing the branching, creeping rhizome in spring or, if you have a greenhouse available, early autumn. Growing from seed, although relatively easy, will not necessarily maintain the original colour, shape or size of the flower. Seed should be collected when ripe (as the seed pods turn brown) and stored ready for sowing in early spring, in a greenhouse, in moist conditions.

Iris ensata 'Variegata'
Variegated Japanese flag

Hardy herbaceous perennial

Natural habitat
Moist ground, drying out in winter

Ideal conditions
Wet ground in summer, drier in winter

Ideal planting depth
5cm (2in) above to soil at water level

Light requirements
Full sun to partial shade

Soil preference
Medium loam with plenty of humus and nutrients

Flower type
Single flowers with three petals

Flower colour
Deep purple

Flowering time
Early to midsummer

Normal height
Up to 90cm (3ft)

Propagation
By division of rhizomes in spring or early autumn

Particulars

This variegated cultivar of *Iris ensata* is truly beautiful. Its deep purple blooms stand out clearly against the tall, vertical, green-and-white, spear-shaped leaves. Although not truly aquatic, it should be part of any collection: the foliage provides colour all season long, with the beautiful flowers adding more in summer.

As said, this is not strictly an aquatic plant. It does enjoy a wet situation in the summer months but can sometimes suffer – and even die – if left in water through the winter. It needs to dry out to some extent at this time, in a fairly frost-free area, to keep the rhizome fully healthy. For best results, remove the plant from the water in late summer, dig a hole in a spare corner of your garden and sink the plant in, pot and all. Leave it there until late spring, when it will enjoy going back into the water just as its new growth is starting.

Old leaves should be left in place, to prevent ingress of water, and removed in early spring, before the new growth appears. If the leaves are removed before winter, water that collects in the exposed hollow tubes may freeze, breaking the cell walls of the plant and thus killing it. The plant requires the addition of extra food every spring, or weak foliage and flower will result. Additional food should be provided in spring or weak foliage and poor flowers will result.

Propagation is best done by division of the branching, creeping rhizome in spring or, if a greenhouse is available, early autumn. Growing from seed, although relatively easy, will not necessarily maintain the original colour, shape or size of the flower. Seed should be collected when ripe (as the seed pods turn brown) and stored ready for sowing in early spring, in a greenhouse, in moist conditions.

Iris 'Gerald Darby'
Purple-stemmed water iris

True aquatic; Hardy herbaceous perennial

Natural habitat
Wetlands and banks of lakes, rivers and streams

Ideal conditions
Shallow water

Ideal planting depth
0–20cm (0–8in) below water

Light requirements
Full sun to partial shade

Soil preference
Heavy loam to clay

Normal height
60–80cm (2–2½ft)

Flower type
Single with three petals

Flower colour
Blue-mauve with yellow-and-white streaked throat

Flowering time
Early to midsummer

Propagation
By division of roots or seed from mid- to late spring

Particulars
Iris 'Gerald Darby' is the successful result of a somewhat obscure cross between several genera, including *I. versicolor* and *I. robusta* (it is also known as *I. x robusta* 'Gerald Darby'). A true water iris, this cultivar thrives in a shallow-water environment. It has a blue-mauve flower with a white-and-yellow streaked throat and purple flower stems.

Caring for this plant involves the removal of old foliage to avoid overcrowding and pollution of the pond from rotting leaves. Additional food is not usually required as the plant generally feeds off the pond water. However, if the plant appears weak and spindly and does not flower, add some slow-release fertilizer.

'Gerald Darby' can be quite a vigorous plant. The creeping rhizomes should be trimmed back occasionally to maintain some control. By far the best approach is to leave the plant for two or three seasons then remove it, divide the rhizomes, and re-pot the resultant splits. This will maintain the health and vigour of the plant *and* provide you with additional plants.

This division is the simplest and easiest way to obtain new plants. Seedlings will not only take at least two years to produce flowers but the resultant plants may not be true to their parent; a divided plant will flower the following year and will be true.

Seeds, if you wish to have a go, should be gathered when ripe. The pods will turn light brown and open up to reveal reddish brown seeds. Store until late autumn, then plant in good heavy loam, cover lightly, and leave outside in moist conditions until germination the following spring. Prick out when about 5cm (2in) tall.

Iris laevigata cultivars ('Snowdrift' shown below)
Japanese water iris

True aquatic; Hardy herbaceous perennial

Natural habitat
Marshy margins of natural lakes and ponds

Ideal conditions
Marshy ground to shallow water

Ideal planting depth
0–10cm (0–4in) below water

Light requirements
Prefers full sun but will tolerate partial shade

Soil preference
Heavy loam to clay

Normal height
Up to 80cm (2½ft)

Flower type
Single with three petals

Flower colour
Blue

Flowering time
Early to midsummer

Propagation
By division of rhizomes or seed from mid- to late spring

Particulars
Iris laevigata is graced with mid-blue flowers, but the colours of its many cultivars include pure white, red, pink, pale blue and royal blue. *Iris laevigata* is three-petalled, but there are five-petalled cultivars such as *I. laevigata* 'Snowdrift', which has pure white, five-petalled blooms with a yellow blaze in the throat. This plant is magnificent, but hard to come by. All *I. laevigata* cultivars are true water irises and love a wet environment.

They need no extra care or attention other than for their excess growth to be trimmed back at the end of the growing season. They are quite capable of drawing all the nutrients they require from their surroundings. All can be quite vigorous under most circumstances. They should be divided at least once every three years, to maintain the health of the plant.

Propagation is best carried out by division as, when growing from seed, you can never be sure of the flower colour on the resultant plants. Seed should be collected as soon as it is ripe; the pods will turn light brown and open to reveal reddish-brown seeds. Store until late autumn, then plant in good heavy loam, cover lightly, and leave outside in moist conditions until germination the following spring. Prick out when about 5cm (2in) tall.

Iris laevigata 'Variegata'
Variegated Japanese water iris

True aquatic; Hardy herbaceous perennial

Natural habitat
Marshy margins of natural lakes and ponds

Ideal conditions
Marshy ground to shallow water

Ideal planting depth
0–10cm (0–4in) below water

Light requirements
Prefers full sun but will tolerate partial shade

Soil preference
Heavy loam to clay

Normal height
Up to 80cm (2½ft)

Flower type
Single with three petals

Flower colour
Light blue

Flowering time
Early to midsummer

Propagation
By division of rhizomes from mid- to late spring

Particulars
Iris laevigata 'Variegata' is magnificent but hard to come by, and usually isn't cheap, but the beauty of this iris rivals even that of *I. ensata* 'Variegata'. It has relatively broad, elongated, spear-shaped leaves with even bands of creamy white and soft mid-green. This variegation tends to fade a little at the height of summer, as with all variegated irises. The beautiful powder blue flowers appear in succession, from early to midsummer, rising from amongst the leaves on tall stems. On a mature plant, the flowers will last two or three weeks.

All *I. laevigata* cultivars are true water irises and love a wet environment. They need no extra care or attention other than trimming back excess growth at the end of the season.

While 'Variegata' is not quite as vigorous as other cultivars, it should still be divided at least once every three years, to maintain the health of the plant. Little extra care is needed as the plant is quite capable of drawing all the nutrients it requires from its surroundings.

Division is also the best method for propagation. Growing from seed is uncertain; the new plants will revert to plain leaves more often than not. However, should you wish to try, seed should be collected as soon as it is ripe; the pods will turn light brown and open to reveal reddish-brown seeds. Store until late autumn, plant in good heavy loam, cover lightly, and leave outside in moist conditions until germination the following spring. Prick out when about 5cm (2in) tall.

Iris pseudacorus
Yellow flag

Hardy herbaceous perennial

Natural habitat
Marshy ground, banks of rivers, lakes and ponds

Ideal conditions
From marshy ground to 20cm (8in) or more below water level

Ideal planting depth
0–20cm (0–8in) below water

Light requirements
Full sun to partial shade

Soil preference
Heavy loam to clay

Normal height
1m (3ft)

Flower type
Single with three petals

Flower colour
Golden yellow

Flowering time
Early to midsummer

Propagation
By division of rhizomes or seed

Particulars
Yellow flag can be seen growing in most wetlands, the bold splashes of golden yellow flowers standing out from the lush vegetation surrounding it.

Totally at home in an aquatic environment, often growing in relatively deep water, it is capable of taking considerable abuse as regards planting depths. Yellow flag is a voracious feeder in order to meet its rapid growing habit. This, if space allows, makes it very effective at vegetable filtration and controlling water clarity.

The only care required is control. As it is very vigorous, steps should be taken to ensure that it does not take over. Mature plants should be cut back annually to maintain control. If you are wary of damaging the pond liner with a knife, snap off a section of the rhizome for greater access and more freedom of movement.

Should the need arise, yellow flag will grow readily from seed – just plant the ripened seed outdoors in a moist situation, and wait for germination in spring. Generally all that is needed is to plant the trimmed sections of rhizome into new pots.

67

Iris pseudacorus 'Variegata'
Variegated yellow flag

True aquatic; Hardy herbaceous perennial

Natural habitat
Marshy ground, banks of rivers, lakes and ponds

Ideal conditions
From marshy ground to 10cm (4in) or more below water level

Ideal planting depth
0–20cm (0–8in) below water

Light requirements
Full sun to partial shade

Soil preference
Heavy loam to clay

Normal height
1m (3ft)

Flower type
Single with three petals

Flower colour
Golden yellow

Flowering time
Early to midsummer

Propagation
By division of rhizomes or seed from mid- to late spring

Particulars
The variegated yellow flag is totally at home in an aquatic environment and is often seen growing in relatively deep water; it is capable of taking considerable abuse as regards planting depths. The vertical variegation is an almost fifty/fifty division of creamy yellow and green along the whole length of the elongated, spear-shaped leaf. This variegation is more pronounced early in the year – as the sun climbs higher, the variegation tends to fade, becoming quite difficult to see at times. The golden yellow flower is, if anything, a little paler than the basic yellow flag, but attractive nonetheless.

The only care this plant requires is control. It can be quite vigorous so steps should be taken to ensure that it does not take over. Mature plants should be cut back annually to maintain control. If you are wary of damaging the pond liner with a knife, snap off a section of the rhizome to give you less restricted access and thus more freedom of movement and control.

Variegated yellow flag will grow readily from seed but don't expect to get variegated plants in return for your efforts as the new plants invariably revert to plain green – you will be lucky to get a few variegated plants from several hundred seeds. If you do wish to follow this road, just plant ripened seed outdoors in a moist situation, and wait for spring. For division, the most reliable method of propagation, all that is needed is to plant the trimmed sections of rhizome into new pots.

Iris sibirica and cultivars (*Iris sibirica* shown below)
Siberian flag

Hardy herbaceous perennial

Natural habitat
Moist ground bordering natural wetlands

Ideal conditions
Moist ground that is rich in organic matter

Ideal planting depth
7.5cm (3in) above to soil at water

Light requirements
Prefers full sun but will tolerate partial shade

Soil preference
Rich, moist soil to normal garden loam

Normal height
60–80cm (2–2½ft)

Flower type
Single with three petals

Flower colour
Blue, and many different coloured cultivars

Flowering time
Early to midsummer

Propagation
By division of roots from mid- to late spring

Particulars
Though occurring mainly in central and eastern Europe, *Iris sibirica* and its cultivars, as the name suggests, can also be found as far north as Siberia. This genus is vastly under-publicized and underrated for use in water gardening. The cultivars show considerable variation in colour and form, ranging through all shades of blue to white and red, with many shades in between. Perhaps, in time, we will see more of this beautiful plant.

The narrow, grassy foliage grows to a height of 80cm (2½ft) or so, from a clump-forming root system that is not too vigorous. Fortunately, it lacks the tendency to take over that many irises have: the root system is more bulbous in habit than the thick, sprawling rhizomes of all the other pond irises.

The *sibiricas* do not enjoy being totally submerged, having evolved in a habitat where the crown of the plant is usually above the mean water level – in marshy to moist ground – as opposed to a water environment. If you bear this in mind, *sibiricas* are very easy to grow but if they are too wet they can suffer, a poor showing of foliage and flowers being the result. In extreme conditions, where the crown (or soil level) is well below the water level for long periods, they may die.

These plants appreciate additional food every year: a lack of food results in fewer flowers. A few teaspoonfuls of bone meal, or other proprietary fertilizer, in pellet form, will satisfy their needs.

To propagate *sibiricas*, it is best to divide the root clumps every three years. Being very dense, you will need two strong forks to prise them apart. Plant divided root clumps in good garden loam with a little extra fertilizer and place in a situation where the bottom third of the pot is in water. Once the plants are well established, the pots can be placed a little deeper. They don't always set seed and seed cannot be relied upon for general propagation purposes, unless you pollinate by hand.

69

Iris versicolor and cultivars (*Iris versicolor* shown below)
Blue flag/wild iris/American water iris

True aquatic; Hardy herbaceous perennial

Natural habitat
Wetlands

Ideal conditions
Shallow water

Ideal planting depth
0–20cm (0–8in) below water

Light requirements
Full sun to partial shade

Soil preference
Heavy loam to clay

Normal height
60–80cm (2–2½ft)

Flower type
Single with three petals

Flower colour
Varying shades of mauve with bold yellow-and-white throat

Flowering time
Early to midsummer

Propagation
By division of roots from mid- to late spring or seed

Particulars
Iris versicolor and its cultivars are true water irises; they thrive in a shallow water environment. *Iris versicolor* has deep mauve flowers with a yellow-and-white throat; the colours of the many different cultivars range from mauve through to pink and beyond. Most of them, unfortunately, are quite rare and hard to find.

These irises are quite vigorous plants. Their creeping rhizomes should be trimmed back occasionally to maintain some control. It is best to leave the plant for two or three seasons, then remove it, divide, and re-pot the resultant splits. This will maintain the health and vigour of the plant and provide you with additional plants.

Old foliage should be removed to avoid pollution of the pond and overcrowding. Extra food isn't usually required, however, if there is a lack of flowers, and the leaves are weak and yellowing, a little bone meal would be appreciated.

Division of the rhizome is the simplest way to obtain new plants. Seedlings will take at least two years to produce flowers whilst a divided plant will flower the following year. Seeds should be gathered when ripe; the pods will turn light brown and open to reveal reddish-brown seeds. Store seeds until late autumn, then plant them in good heavy loam, cover lightly, and leave outside in moist conditions. They will germinate the following spring. Prick out when about 5cm (2in) tall.

Isolepis cernua (syn. *Scirpus cernuus*)
Miniature rush

Hardy herbaceous perennial

Natural habitat
Marshy, damp areas

Ideal conditions
Moist

Ideal planting depth
5cm (2in) above to 2.5cm (1in) below water

Light requirements
Full sun to partial shade

Soil preference
Not fussy

Normal height
15cm (6in)

Flower type
No significant flower; pubescent seed head

Flower colour
White, insignificant; brown seed head

Flowering time
No significant flower; seed heads in midsummer

Propagation
By division of roots

Particulars
Far too little is seen of this beautiful, small, grass-like rush. It is a very pretty plant. Tiny, tufty, creamy white seed heads appear at the top of very thin, light green, grass-like stems from early to midsummer. These provide a lovely show, nodding in the breeze. The seed heads turn a light brown as they ripen, losing the overall decorative effect.

Although a rush, this plant looks more like a grass and is often seen as a decorative indoor plant. It is fully hardy, with a clump-forming root system that is not invasive. Providing it is kept damp, the plant can easily be grown indoors, in a well-lit spot. In this situation it will not grow over-large, but will still provide colour. If used for indoor decoration, in a moist situation, a good peat-based compost is quite adequate, and the plant will grow well in it. If kept outside near a pond, it will require a little food – bone meal will suffice.

Overall, this is a very easy plant to keep and look after, and is ideal for the small pond or water feature.

Propagation is achieved by dividing the root clump, which is easily split by hand. One mature plant will provide several new ones. The divided plants can be potted in any good loam-based medium.

Juncus ensifolius
Dwarf rush

Hardy herbaceous perennial

Natural habitat
Marshy ground

Ideal conditions
Non-submerged, in shallow water

Ideal planting depth
0–2.5cm (0–1in) below water

Light requirements
Full sun to partial shade

Soil preference
Loam with high humus content

Normal height
15–20cm (6–8in)

Flower type
No significant flower

Flower colour
No significant flower; dark brown, globular seed head

Flowering time
No significant flower; seed heads appear in early summer

Propagation
By seed or division of roots

Particulars

This delightful little rush has a soft, grassy appearance. Its light green, sword-shaped leaves arch gently out from a central root mass to provide massed foliage of no more than 20cm (8in) in height. The dark brown, globe-like seed head starts to show its form in early summer, gradually expanding in size to reach 6–8mm (¼–⅜in) in diameter by late summer, when the ripened seeds have reached full size.

The plant's natural habitat is bog and marsh, so it follows that it enjoys slightly more peat in its planting medium than many other plants. However, as noted in Chapter 2, peat should be avoided in a pond situation. It is a plant that is easy to please and will grow quite happily in good garden loam.

Juncus ensifolius does not have a particularly invasive root system and in that respect, is ideal for the smaller pond. However, its seeds are a different matter; if not removed before they ripen, in late summer, they have a strong tendency to self-seed. The very small seed travels short distances on any breeze, and will gradually colonize the surrounding area, just as it would do in its natural habitat.

The removal of old foliage is about all that is required for this plant; it is more or less self-sufficient in all respects other than that large clumps require division as they will eventually start to die out from the centre.

Given its self-seeding habit, it stands to reason that a good way to propagate this plant is by seed. If you want thousands of plants and are prepared for a very fiddly task then yes; the resultant seedlings are small and quite delicate. But for everyday purposes by far the best method, and the quickest, is to divide mature clumps. The clumps part fairly easily and make healthy new plants a lot sooner than seedlings would.

Juncus spiralis
Corkscrew rush

Hardy evergreen

Natural habitat
Marshy ground

Ideal conditions
Marshy ground, water to top of soil

Ideal planting depth
5cm (2in) above to soil at surface level

Light requirements
Full sun to partial shade

Soil preference
Heavy soil to light clay

Normal height
20–25cm (8–10in)

Flower type
No significant flower

Flower colour
No significant flower; light brown seed head

Flowering time
No significant flower; seed heads from mid-to late summer

Propagation
By seed or division of roots

Particulars
This plant is becoming quite popular throughout horticulture. For some reason it is often called a twisted bamboo, which it isn't. It can be grown almost anywhere that can be kept moist. Its heavily contorted, dark green, cylindrical foliage reaches a full height of about 20cm (8in), maybe a little more in very warm conditions. The plant is fully hardy and evergreen – its leaves look very attractive covered with a winter frost.

A common mistake in siting this plant is to place it in a situation where the crown is well below water level; in this depth of water it will often die. You should always bear in mind that the plant evolved in marshland habitats, where it would get perhaps the occasional ducking, but no prolonged submersion.

Juncus spiralis is fairly undemanding and requires little care, being quite capable of drawing all it needs from its surroundings.

The plant is clump forming and non-invasive. Given the chance it will self-seed, so it is best to remove the seed heads before they ripen in late summer. Ripened seeds should be sown immediately after collection, in moist conditions, where they will germinate steadily after three to four weeks. Not all seedlings will produce new corkscrew rushes; some will revert to *Juncus effussis*, the vertical species of this genus. The wiry root system is quite easily prised apart and will provide several plants at a time, which is usually enough for general purposes.

Jussiaea grandiflora
Flowering ludwigia

Hardy herbaceous perennial

Natural habitat
Wetlands

Ideal conditions
Shallow water

Ideal planting depth
0–30cm (0–12in) below water

Light requirements
Full sun

Soil preference
Heavy loam to clay

Normal height
10–15cm (4–6in)

Flower type
Single, trumpet-like

Flower colour
Deep gold

Flowering time
Late summer

Propagation
By stem cuttings

Particulars
I first saw this attractive, low-scrambling plant – growing around the muddy, semi-dried surrounds of a lake in southern France – some 18 years ago. Not only was it blanketed with beautiful, deep golden flowers, it also covered a considerable area.

With its propensity to crawl and climb anywhere that is moist, *Jussiaea grandiflora* is ideal for concealing unsightly pond edges. It has the ability to survive, even grow and thrive, in water up to 1m (3ft) deep, and will flower only when it reaches the surface. It is quite tough and will survive the winter, particularly if the main root clump is well below water; the colder the winter, the deeper the pot should be.

This plant is a late starter, betraying its origins in warmer climes. It starts to show leaf only in early summer but once it gets going, it grows rapidly. Its flowering period is a little later than many other pond plants making it a welcome addition: it adds colour when colour could well be lacking.

Although it is very pretty when in flower, *J. grandiflora* does require some control to ensure that it doesn't invade indiscriminately. Control is easily maintained by trimming back new growth and removing very long, old stems. These old stems should be removed in late autumn whilst they can still be seen amongst other growth.

The trimmings can be used for propagation, producing more of the same. The plant does not seem to set viable seed in colder climes.

Lobelia 'Queen Victoria'
(No common name)

Hardy herbaceous perennial

Natural habitat
Moist ground, herbaceous borders

Ideal conditions
Moist to wet conditions

Ideal planting depth
5cm (2in) above to 5cm (2in) below water

Light requirements
Full sun

Soil preference
Good garden loam

Normal height
60–80cm (2–2½ft)

Flower type
Labiate, single, semi-pendulous and trumpet-like

Flower colour
Scarlet

Flowering time
Late summer

Propagation
By seed or division of crown

Particulars
Lobelia 'Queen Victoria' is often called *Lobelia cardinalis* or *Lobelia fulgens*; these are, in fact, distinct plants. The actual *Lobelia cardinalis* has green foliage as opposed to the bronze/deep red of *L.* 'Queen Victoria' and *L.* fulgens. 'Queen Victoria' is extremely popular because of the deep red of its mature foliage and its bright scarlet flowers which appear, on tall panicles, in late summer.

This species is quite tolerant; a mature plant will grow happily in water up to 10cm (4in) deep, though young plants need to be acclimatized gradually, as they grow; planting too deep too soon may cause them to die.

'Queen Victoria' is dearly loved by slugs. Place the plant well away from the pond's edge to avoid losing it overnight. The plant is fully hardy, but stems should not be removed before winter. If they are cut back, water may settle in the hollow stems, penetrate the upper part of the crown, freeze and kill the plant. This is one of the main reasons for lost plants; the other, already mentioned, is slugs. Within reason, the more food this plant receives, the larger the plant and its flowers will be. A starved plant will have quite spindly stems, whilst a well-fed one may have stems of 2cm (¾in) or more in diameter.

Mature plants can be divided in spring. One plant will produce two or three new ones at least every other year. Growing from seed is relatively easy. Collect seed when ripe, in early autumn, store until spring and sow, without cover and in moist conditions, in a warm greenhouse. Prick out when large enough to handle and grow on until large enough to place in the pond.

Lobelia siphilitica
Blue lobelia

Hardy herbaceous perennial

Natural habitat
Moist ground, herbaceous borders

Ideal conditions
Moist to wet conditions

Ideal planting depth
5cm (2in) above to 2.5cm (1in) below water

Light requirements
Full sun

Soil preference
Good garden loam

Normal height
60–80cm (2–2½ft)

Flower type
Labiate, single, semi-pendulous and trumpet-like

Flower colour
Sky blue

Flowering time
Late summer

Propagation
By seed or division of crown

Particulars
Lobelia siphilitica has soft, pale green, elliptic foliage borne on central stems. Its sky blue, white-throated flowers appear on the top third of tall panicles in late summer. A mature clump will provide a good show of colour for several weeks. A white-flowering cultivar, *L. s.* 'Alba', is sometimes available. Apart from the flower colour, it has the same characteristics.

Blue lobelia is quite tolerant, with mature plants growing happily in water and in semi-dry conditions, though young plants require gradual acclimatization as they grow; planting too deep too soon may well cause them to die. They have a slowly expanding, clump-forming root system, so are not invasive.

The plant is fully hardy but stems should not be removed before winter: if they are cut back, water may settle in the hollow stems, penetrate the upper part of the crown, freeze and kill the plant. This is the cause of many a lost plant. Within reason, the more food this plant receives, the larger the plant and its flowers will be. A starved plant will have quite spindly stems, whilst a well-fed plant may have stems of 2cm (¾in) or more in diameter.

Mature plants can be divided in spring; one plant will produce two or three new ones at least every other year. Growing from seed is relatively easy. Collect seed when ripe, in early autumn, store until spring and sow, without cover and in moist conditions, in a warm greenhouse. Prick out when large enough to handle, and grow on until large enough to place in the pond.

Lobelia vedrariensis
Mauve lobelia

Hardy herbaceous perennial

Natural habitat
Moist ground, herbaceous borders

Ideal conditions
Moist to wet conditions

Ideal planting depth
5cm (2in) above to 2.5cm (1in) below water

Light requirements
Full sun

Soil preference
Good garden loam

Normal height
60–80cm (2–2½ft)

Flower type
Labiate, single, semi-pendulous and trumpet-like

Flower colour
Dark blue to mauve

Flowering time
Late summer

Propagation
By seed or division of crown

Particulars
Lobelia vedrariensis has dark green, elliptic foliage borne on tall, central stems. The flowers have white streaks on their throat. They appear in succession along the top third of tall panicles, in late summer. A mature clump will provide a splendid show of colour for several weeks.

Mauve lobelia is quite water tolerant, and mature plants will grow happily in water and in semi-dry conditions. Young plants, on the other hand, require gradual acclimatization as they grow; planting too deep too soon may well cause them to die. They have a slowly expanding, clump-forming root system, so are not invasive.

The plant is fully hardy but stems should not be removed before winter: if they are cut back, water may settle in the hollow stems, penetrate the upper part of the crown, freeze and kill the plant. This is the cause of many a lost plant. Within reason, the more food this plant receives, the larger the plant and its flowers will be. A starved plant will have quite spindly stems, whilst a well-fed plant may have stems of 2cm (¾in) or more in diameter.

Mature plants can be divided in spring; one plant will produce two or three new ones at least every other year. Growing from seed is relatively easy. Collect seed when ripe, in early autumn, store until spring and sow, without cover and in moist conditions, in a warm greenhouse. Prick out when large enough to handle, and grow on until large enough to place in the pond.

Lysichiton americanus
Yellow skunk cabbage

Hardy herbaceous perennial

Natural habitat
Marshy ground bordering natural lakes and streams

Ideal conditions
Marshy ground

Ideal planting depth
0–5cm (0–2in) below water

Light requirements
Partial shade

Soil preference
Heavy loam to clay

Normal height
1m (3ft) plus

Flower type
Spathe

Flower colour
Yellow

Flowering time
Late spring to early summer

Propagation
By seed

Particulars
Yellow skunk cabbage certainly lives up to its name; the leaves especially exude a foetid aroma, more so when brushed against or bruised. This native of North America is very noticeable in an enclosed space.

It is a striking, bold plant ideally suited to large lakes or natural settings.

The plant is generally too large for the average garden pond. It requires a large, deep pot to contain and support the probing tap-root system – this reaches considerable depths in a natural environment. It also needs a large container to prevent it blowing over; the large, paddle-like leaves certainly catch the wind.

Spathe-like flowers of about 30cm (12in) appear in late spring before many of the leaves have formed. These flowers are discarded after the large cylindrical seed pods have formed. Leaves reach their full size by early summer and last well into early autumn.

Damaged and old leaves should be removed as and when required. In artificial conditions this plant will require additional food to thrive. It is what is called a gross feeder, requiring a great deal of food to support the mass of dark green leaves it produces throughout the season.

The rather large seed pods ripen slowly, softening continually until they fall apart to lie on the ground, revealing a glutinous mass of seed and pith. Seeds should be gathered and planted in heavy, moist soil and left until spring, then moved to a warm area where gradual germination will take place, with young plants appearing by midsummer.

Lysichiton camtschatcensis
Asian skunk cabbage

Hardy herbaceous perennial

Natural habitat
Marshy ground bordering natural lakes and streams

Ideal conditions
Marshy ground

Ideal planting depth
0–5cm (0–2in) below water

Light requirements
Partial shade

Soil preference
Heavy loam to clay

Normal height
1m (3ft)

Flower type
Spathe

Flower colour
White

Flowering time
Late spring to early summer

Propagation
By seed

Particulars

The Asian skunk cabbage lives up to its name too. As with yellow skunk cabbage, the leaves especially exude a foetid aroma, more so when brushed against or bruised. This native of eastern Asia is very noticeable in an enclosed space. It is a striking, bold plant ideally suited to large lakes or natural settings.

The plant is generally too large for the average garden pond. It requires a large, deep pot to contain and support the probing tap-root system – this reaches considerable depths in a natural environment. It also needs a large container to prevent it blowing over; the large, paddle-like leaves certainly catch the wind.

Spathe-like flowers of about 25cm (10in) appear in late spring before many of the leaves have formed. It flowers a little later than its North American relative (see p 78) and its flowers are a little smaller. They are discarded after the almost pointed, cylindrical seed pod has formed. Leaves reach their full size by early summer and last well into early autumn. Damaged and old leaves should be removed as and when required. This plant requires additional food to thrive in artificial conditions. It is what is called a gross feeder, requiring a great deal of food to support the mass of dark green leaves it produces throughout the season.

The seed pods ripen slowly, softening continually until they fall apart to lie on the ground, revealing a glutinous mass of seed and pith. Seeds should be gathered and planted in heavy, moist soil and left until spring, then moved to a warm area where gradual germination will take place. Young plants will appear by midsummer. If you wish to grow from seed, ensure that the plant is not near a *Lysichiton americanus*: insects will cross pollinate them, giving you a green-tinged flower rather than its true snow white.

79

Lysimachia nummularia
Creeping jenny

Hardy herbaceous perennial

Natural habitat
Moist

Ideal conditions
Moist ground

Ideal planting depth
0–2.5cm (0–1in) below water

Light requirements
Full sun, shade tolerant

Soil preference
Good garden loam

Normal height
5cm (2in)

Flower type
Single, open cup

Flower colour
Yellow

Flowering time
Summer

Propagation
By stem cuttings

Particulars
This creeping, ground-hugging plant has crossed over from the range of drier garden plants. It loves a damp to wet environment and on occasion will grow right out into the pond. It is ideal for concealing unsightly areas. The light green, elliptic leaves sprout alternately from slender, multibranched stems. These can reach considerable lengths over a growing season.

The cultivar *Lysimachia nummularia* 'Aurea' has the same characteristics but with yellow leaves and flowers.

The plant is fully hardy in all but extreme winter conditions. Control should be exercised by trimming back excess growth as required. Little other care is required; it is very self-sufficient.

Propagation is simplicity itself; plant up short lengths of stem in warm, moist conditions. Within a week or two, these will have rooted and new plants will form.

Lythrum salicaria
Purple loosestrife

Hardy herbaceous perennial

Natural habitat
Moist, marshy ground, natural wetlands

Ideal conditions
Good soil, very moist to wet ground, full sun

Ideal planting depth
0–5cm (0–2in) below water

Light requirements
Full sun to partial shade

Soil preference
Heavy loam

Normal height
Up to 1.5m (4½ft)

Flower type
Clustered single flowers on pannicles

Flowering time
Midsummer

Flower colour
Dark pink to red

Propagation
By seed

Particulars
Purple loosestrife flowers in large drifts on wasteland and wetlands. The plant develops tall, woody stems that can reach heights of 1.5m (4½ft) or more under ideal conditions. The drier the ground, the smaller the plant, but this extremely tough plant will still grow, even with little moisture available. Bold masses of small, dark pink flowers adorn at least the top third of every multibranched stem, providing an excellent show of colour for two to three weeks and sometimes more.

The plant is a prolific self-seeder, so care must be taken to remove old flower stems before the seeds have a chance to ripen – in late summer – and scatter in the breeze. Once established, this plant requires little care other than this. Old, woody stems should be cut right down before spring; new green shoots appear in late spring and grow quite rapidly through early summer.

Propagation from seed is extremely easy; collect a stem on which the seed pods have turned brown, shake over a tray of moist compost, and leave in warm spot. Keep moist and all too soon you will have more plants than you need. **81**

Mentha aquatica
Water mint

True aquatic; Hardy herbaceous perennial

Natural habitat
Natural wetlands, borders and banks of streams, rivers and lakes

Ideal conditions
Marshy

Ideal planting depth
5cm (2in) above to 5cm (2in) below water

Light requirements
Full sun to partial shade

Soil preference
Wide range of soils, from heavy loam to quite a high humus content

Normal height
45cm (1½ft)

Flower type
Globular cluster of tiny single flowers

Flower colour
Light mauve

Flowering time
Mid- to late summer

Propagation
By stem cuttings

Particulars
Water mint has a definite minty aroma, particularly when brushed against or crushed. Used in cooking, its flavour is a lot stronger than that of normal garden mint. Distinctive globular clusters of tiny mauve flowers appear from among the leaves from mid- to late summer. These last several weeks, with large clumps producing a bold show of colour.

The plant scrambles over moist ground by means of a creeping, ground-hugging horizontal stem. It sends up almost square, purple-green stems at intervals along its ever-increasing length. This stem roots very readily – from each leaf node – wherever it finds soil. In a pond situation these stems often become sub-aquatic, moving through deeper water to emerge unexpectedly, some distance from the main plant. Because of this habit, care must be taken to ensure that it doesn't colonize large areas uninvited. Trimming, or nipping back stems as you see them, will usually suffice. Little other care is required.

Trimmings can be used to propagate new plants should you desire them. The plant does produce seed, but the seed is so fine it is hard to see, making collection difficult, and as the plant is so prolific, this is rarely necessary.

Mentha cervina (previously known as *Preslia cervina*)
Water spearmint

Hardy herbaceous perennial

Ideal conditions
Moist to wet ground

Ideal planting depth
2.5cm (1in) above to 2.5cm (1in) below water

Natural habitat
Moist ground

Light requirements
Full sun

Soil preference
Not fussy as long as not too alkaline

Normal height
30cm (12in)

Flower type
Globe-like, clustered, small, single

Flower colour
Lavender

Flowering time
Summer

Propagation
By stem cuttings

Particulars

This very aromatic mint is somewhat less well-known than *Mentha aquatica* but has the advantage of being non-invasive as the growth of both its foliage and root system is not too vigorous. This makes it ideal for any pond, large or small. The plant has erect stems that support quite small and slender, light green, elliptic leaves along their full length. These decrease in size as they near the top, giving a slender, pyramid effect. Clustered, globular, lavender flowers appear from the leaf nodes up the length of the stem, from early to midsummer, in succession. Both the flower and foliage of this plant retain their aroma, even when dried, making it a welcome addition – in small quantities – to pot-pourri.

There is a white-flowered subspecies of this plant, *Mentha cervina alba*, which is the same in all respects except for the colour of its flower.

Little care is required other than the removal of dead and dying old foliage.

Propagation by stem cuttings is extremely easy. Short pieces of young stem pushed into moist soil, and kept in warm conditions, will soon root and grow away after two or three weeks.

83

Mentha pulegium
Pennyroyal

Hardy herbaceous perennial

Natural habitat
Normal to moist ground anywhere

Ideal conditions
Moist

Ideal planting depth
5cm (2in) above to water level

Light requirements
Full sun to partial shade

Soil preference
Wide range of soils, from garden loam to moist areas with quite a high humus content

Normal height
2.5cm (1in)

Flower type
Small clusters of tiny, single flowers

Flower colour
Light mauve

Flowering time
Mid- to late summer

Propagation
By stem cuttings

Particulars
This little mint scrambles over the ground by means of delicate, creeping, ground-hugging, horizontal stems. These are covered with small, light green, elliptic leaves. It is another plant that has crossed over from the normal garden plant range and thoroughly enjoys the moist conditions. A prolific plant, it is ideal for ground cover in a pond environment, as it covers all the soil it encounters and will even travel through shallow water to carpet soil at some distance from the main plant.

The multibranched stems root very readily, from each leaf node, wherever they find soil, so care must be taken to ensure that it doesn't colonize large areas, unless you want it to. Trimming, or nipping back these stems as you see them will usually suffice. Little care, other than controlling its prolific growth, is required, though the removal of dead leaves prior to winter is advisable in order to reduce the risk of pollution.

Trimmings can be used to propagate new plants should you wish to do so.

Menyanthes trifoliata
Bog bean/buckbean

True aquatic; Hardy herbaceous perennial

Natural habitat
Shallow margins of natural bodies of water

Ideal conditions
Shallow water

Ideal planting depth
0–20cm (0–8in) below water

Light requirements
Full sun to dappled shade

Soil preference
Heavy loam to clay

Normal height
15cm (6in)

Flower type
Single, clustered, star-like and fringed

Flower colour
Blushed white, tinged with red on the outside

Flowering time
Late spring to early summer

Propagation
By cuttings or division of stems

Particulars

This is a curious – and somewhat untidy – low, scrambling plant. In the space of a few years, it will colonize considerable areas. The dark green, cylindrical, horizontal stems are somewhat bamboo-like in appearance, with circular nodes at regular intervals along their length. Its sprawling, creeping habit can be useful for concealing unsightly areas; branching stems will find their way amongst the stems of other, taller plants growing in the margins. Water-loving, these stems readily send out aerial roots that feed off the water.

The three-lobed, ovate leaves, akin to a broad bean leaf, are supported on short stems, as are the fringed, star-like flowers that appear from late spring to early summer. The reddish, clustered buds, appearing well before the flowers themselves open, are attractive in their own right.

The only care required is growth control; trim back excess and old growth as necessary. The plant is very self-sufficient in all other respects.

The aerial rooted stems are ideal for propagation purposes; simply remove them from the parent plant, pot horizontally, and submerge straight away.

Mimulus cardinalis
Cardinal flower

Half-hardy herbaceous perennial

Natural habitat
Moist ground

Ideal conditions
Water to soil level or moist ground

Ideal planting depth
0–2.5cm (0–1in) below water

Light requirements
Full sun

Soil preference
Good, well-fertilized loam

Normal height
45cm (1½ft)

Flower type
Labiate, snapdragon-like

Flower colour
Bright red

Flowering time
Summer

Propagation
By seed or division of roots

Particulars
Mimulus cardinalis has attractive, soft green, downy (pubescent) leaves borne on a light green, cylindrical stem that reaches about 45cm (*1½ft*) in height. The bright red, almost scarlet flowers are quite large and labiate. They appear throughout midsummer; at the same time, the plant begins to look a little untidy.

Once flowering is over, cut the plant back to encourage new, more attractive growth. In very temperate and warm regions it may even flower again. The plant, although hardy in all but extreme climes, will appreciate additional protection if severe weather is expected: it is susceptible to very low temperatures. In spring extra food, in the form of bone meal, is always welcome and will result in stronger foliage and larger flowers.

Mature plants can be divided in spring, but to be sure of new plants, it is best to collect the very fine seed from ripened seed pods and re-sow in late spring. Scatter on the surface of moist compost and keep in warm conditions. Once started, growth is quite rapid and the plants will quickly be ready for pricking out.

Mimulus luteus
Monkey flower/yellow musk

True aquatic; Hardy herbaceous perennial

Natural habitat
Marshy ground

Ideal conditions
Moist to wet conditions

Ideal planting depth
0–5cm (0–2in) below water

Light requirements
Full sun, though tolerant of shade

Soil preference
Not fussy, will grow wherever it falls

Normal height
30–45cm (12–18in)

Flower type
Labiate, trumpet-like

Flower colour
Yellow, with red marks in throat

Flowering time
From early summer

Propagation
By seed

Particulars
The seeds of this plant do not need much moisture to germinate; the plant is so prolific, it is almost a weed. Nevertheless, it does have its merits – it produces a lovely show of bright yellow-gold flowers from early summer onwards and is such a strong grower that, if cut back right after the first flush of flowers, it will produce more foliage and flower again in a short space of time.

This mimulus is one to be wary of: being a very prolific self-seeder, the unwary can soon have a garden full of it. *Mimulus moschatus*, a very similar plant with smaller, downy, sticky leaves, has the same self-seeding habit and can be a real pest. The ripened seed, very small and light brown, is readily scattered in light breezes. Flower stems should be removed as soon as the flowers are over to avoid extensive colonization.

Another near relative, *Mimulus guttatus*, looks and acts the same in all respects except for its flowers. These have a light scattering of red spots on the throat rather than the two red marks of *M. luteus*. These two are often sold under the other's name due to some confusion over which is which.

The plant does not require additional food. The only care really necessary is control of the seed.

Propagation, should you ever wish to produce more of the plant, is carried out by sprinkling collected seed on moist soil; sit back and wait a week to see results.

Mimulus ringens
Lavender musk

True aquatic; Hardy herbaceous perennial

Natural habitat
Shallow water to marshy ground

Ideal conditions
Moist to wet

Ideal planting depth
0–7.5cm (0–3in) below water

Light requirements
Full sun, though tolerant of shade to some extent

Soil preference
Moisture-laden, heavy loam

Normal height
90cm (3ft)

Flower type
Labiate trumpet

Flower colour
Pale lavender

Flowering time
Midsummer

Propagation
By seed or division

Particulars
Being a true aquatic, *Mimulus ringens* loves an aquatic environment and will grow happily in conditions ranging from shallow water to the muddy margins of natural lakes and ponds.

Its tall, square, almost woody, hollow stems rise from the water to support narrow, elongated, elliptic, mid-green leaves. The pale lavender flowers, though similar in appearance to those of *Mimulus luteus* (see p 87), are somewhat smaller than this near cousin. The plant is not so prolific and is quite easily controlled.

It is best to allow the hollow stems to die off naturally and remove them in early spring, after the frosts, to prevent ice damage to the crown. A little extra food in early spring gives this plant a boost, encouraging much stronger stems and a greater show of flowers in the summer. Because of its height, it is subject to wind damage; some protection, if possible, is beneficial; use it between stronger plants such as iris.

The root system lends itself to division, sending new shoots upwards and outwards from the central crown. These already rooted shoots are easily cropped and planted, providing all the plants you will need for normal purposes.

Myosotis palustris
Water forget-me-not

True aquatic; Hardy herbaceous perennial

Natural habitat
Shallow water, streams, lakes and ponds

Ideal conditions
Shallow water

Ideal planting depth
0–10cm (0–4in) below water

Light requirements
Full sun to partial shade

Soil preference
Not fussy

Normal height
15cm (6in)

Flower type
Single

Flower colour
Blue

Flowering time
Early summer

Propagation
By stem cuttings

Particulars
The soft green leaves of *Myosotis palustris* emerge from the shallows in spring, providing a welcome splash of foliage in what is still a fairly barren waterscape. Mature clumps can carpet large areas, due to the creeping habit of the plant's main stem. It is easily controlled by pulling out unwanted growth. The tiny blue flowers appear in profusion from late spring to early summer. The branching, slender stems appear quite delicate but are almost woody and relatively strong. There are white and pink forms of this plant available. They make take some seeking out as they are not as widely distributed as the blue variety.

Old growth can become straggly and untidy, requiring a good trim and tidy up once flowering is over. Cutting right back to within 2–5cm (1–2in) of the main root system will do this robust plant little harm; it rapidly sends up new growth, perhaps even producing another flush of flowers later in the year. Old stems, if left through the winter, appear black and dead, but leave them and in spring you will see new growth appearing from latent buds formed the previous year, along their whole length.

To propagate, simply take a few healthy pieces of plant that already have a small root system, and submerge, just below the surface, straight away. The plant does produce seed, but it is rarely necessary to harvest it as its natural vegetative growth is so prolific.

Rorippa nasturtium-aquaticum
Watercress

Treat as an annual

Natural habitat
Shallow water in rivers and streams

Ideal conditions
Shallow water

Ideal planting depth
0–10cm (0–4in) below water

Light requirements
Full sun, but will tolerate some shade

Soil preference
Heavy loam to clay

Normal height
Up to 45cm (1½ft)

Flower type
Tiny, clustered, single

Flower colour
White

Flowering time
Summer

Propagation
By seed or stem cuttings

Particulars
This watercress is ideal for those requiring a rapidly feeding plant as a summer filter. It develops a considerable matt of aerially feeding roots along submerged stems, requiring no soil. Pieces broken off these rooted stems will grow away vigorously and quite happily in the tops of vegetative filters or on top of bio filters.

Where it has an abundance of food, the growth rate of this plant is quite phenomenal. Moreover, you can eat it; not only does it help in controlling excess algae, it is great in salads too.

The removal of long, leggy growth is essential to maintain the young, light green, tender foliage. The flowers are a dirty white and though somewhat insignificant individually, they are borne in clusters and in this form, stand out during their brief, but oft-repeated flowering. The fresh young growth of the plant is the most attractive, with the older growth looking very straggly and untidy.

Left to its own devices, the plant will flop over when it gets too tall to support itself, and re-root in fresh areas of soil or develop aerial roots if it falls in water. The plant also self-seeds readily; if you don't want large colonies of cress everywhere, remove old flowers before they produce seed. Old plants should be removed before the onset of winter, to avoid pollution from the mass of vegetation and stems.

To provide new plants in spring, collect the little black seeds from just a few stems, sow them in heavy, wet loam, keep warm and they will soon be ready to plant out wherever needed.

Nymphoides peltata
Water fringe

True aquatic; Hardy herbaceous perennial

Natural habitat
Natural bodies of water

Ideal conditions
Water up to 60cm (2ft) deep

Ideal planting depth
5–45cm (2–18in) below water

Light requirements
Full sun to partial shade

Soil preference
Heavy loam to clay

Normal height
Floating leaves and flowers

Flower colour
Yellow

Flower type
Single, buttercup-like

Flowering time
Summer

Propagation
By stem cuttings

Particulars

Nymphoides peltata also goes by the names villarsia, water fringe and floating heart; by any name, it is a real pest once established, if you are not very careful.

The floating, heart-shaped leaves are mid-green, sometimes with small purplish markings, and 5–7.5cm (2–3in) across. They sprout from a floating, creeping stem system that knows no bounds as far as colonization goes; it will even grow up a muddy bank to set up home.

In summer, when in full flower, it can be an attractive plant but the foliage tends to be so tangled and dense that it blots out the light to all submerged aquatics. Remove as much growth as possible before winter to avoid pollution problems. Providing you are prepared to keep it under control, it can be a valuable provider of early cover and consumer of excess nitrates. If you are not, it is best avoided.

To propagate, cut off a length of already rooted, floating stem and place where required. Keep the shears handy for when it spreads too far.

Oenanthe javanica 'flamingo'

Variegated water celery/pink flamingo

True aquatic; Hardy herbaceous perennial

Natural habitat
Boggy, marshy ground

Ideal conditions
Shallow water to muddy margins

Ideal planting depth
0–10cm (0–4in) below water

Light requirements
Full sun

Soil preference
Not fussy

Normal height
Up to 20cm (8in)

Flower type
No significant flower

Flower colour
No significant flower; grown for its cream, pale green and pinkish red foliage

Flowering time
No significant flower

Propagation
By division of roots or stems

Particulars

This is another true aquatic from North America. It loves very moist to wet conditions. A tough plant, its root system is inclined to be invasive if left to its own devices.

Growth appears as soon as the frosts abate, with daintily coloured deep pink, pale green and creamy white leaves appearing to decorate the pond margins. The leaves are deeply indented and supported by short, very pale green stems.

The extreme paleness of the stems lead some to think the plant is starved of nitrogen but this is not so; it is quite normal and does not require extra food to rectify it.

A welcome addition to the pond, this colourful plant can, at times, get a little straggly. If this happens, the odd trim doesn't go amiss.

Do watch the root system: it can spread unobtrusively and unnoticed until it appears amongst other plants, having invaded their containers from below.

Propagation is just a matter of potting root trimmings and submerging 1cm (⅜in) or so below water.

Orontium aquaticum
Golden club

True aquatic; Hardy herbaceous perennial

Natural habitat
Shallow water bordering natural lakes, rivers and streams

Ideal conditions
Water around 15–20cm (6–8in) deep

Ideal planting depth
15–30cm (6–12in) below water

Light requirements
Full sun

Soil preference
Clay

Normal height
15–20cm (6–8in)

Flower type
Spike-like florets

Flower colour
Gold-and-white

Flowering time
Late spring to early summer

Propagation
By division of roots of mature plants

Particulars
Another true aquatic from North America, this unusual and attractive plant is non-invasive. It has a clump-forming, slowly expanding central crown that eventually produces additional young plants around its circumference. The leaves are a metallic green on the upper surface and somewhat silvery beneath. They float on the water's surface, surrounding the flower stems that appear in late spring. These unusually white flower stems arch gently outwards from the centre of the plant and form a peculiar golden-yellow floret or spike along their top third. These are not flowers in the recognized sense perhaps, but flowers they are. Pollinated by insects, they produce a number of almost black, pea-like seeds by late summer.

The plant has a deep rooting system that requires plenty of deep loamy clay to perform at its best. Give it deep, non-perforated pots with added organic food and you will be well rewarded with a mass of flowers. Remove old and decaying foliage as it appears to avoid pollution.

The warmer your climate, the more likely you are to have fully developed seeds and the more likely you are to be able to germinate those seeds successfully. Germination may also require the use of certain acids to break down inhibitors, but this is a method best left to professional growers. *Orontium aquaticum* is not a particularly fast grower, so don't expect miracles from seedlings – they can take several years to reach flowering maturity. This even applies to division; young plants removed from the parent will take some time to reach maturity.

Phalaris arundinacea var. *picta*
Variegated canary grass/gardener's garters

Hardy herbaceous perennial

Natural habitat
Semi-dry to moist conditions

Ideal conditions
Moist ground wherever it occurs

Ideal planting depth
5cm (2in) above to 5cm (2in) below water

Light requirements
Full sun, but will tolerate some shade

Soil preference
Not fussy

Normal height
60–90cm (2–3ft)

Flower type
No significant flower; grassy seed head

Flower colour
No significant flower; creamy white seed head

Flowering time
No significant flower; grassy seed head in late summer

Propagation
By division of roots

Particulars
Phalaris arundinacea var. *picta* is an attractive plant, grown for its variegated leaves. The young, vertically striped growth is tipped and streaked with pink which fades to white as the leaves grow. Mature growth has even, vertical stripes of green and white. It soon develops an untidy appearance, becoming dotted with leaves that have passed their best. Cut the mass of vegetation down to within a few centimetres (2–3in) of the pot, and you will be rewarded with fresh, young and very attractive growth. This process can be repeated at least twice during the growing season.

The root system of this plant is one to really watch: it is vigorous, strong and invasive, and will send up new shoots in every direction, in whatever medium it can penetrate. Control is everything. Without it, the root system will take over – big time. Although contrary to the general principles of pond management, it is perhaps best to keep this plant in a non-perforated pot, which makes it much easier to control and handle. Foliage should be removed before winter to prevent undue pollution. No additional food is required, as the plant is totally self-sufficient.

Propagation is merely a matter of potting shoots removed from the root system, placing them in a moist spot and watching the results.

Phragmites communis
Norfolk reed

True aquatic; Hardy herbaceous perennial

Natural habitat
Banks of natural bodies of water

Ideal conditions
Shallow water

Ideal planting depth
0–30cm (0–12in) below water

Light requirements
Full sun, but will tolerate some shade

Soil preference
Heavy loam to clay

Normal height
2m (6ft)

Flower type
Fluffy, almost silky head akin to pampas grass

Flower colour
Creamy white turning to light brown

Flowering time
Early summer

Propagation
By division of roots or seed

Particulars
This is not a plant for the lined pond! The stoloniferous, woody, creeping rootstock possesses a sharp point at the tip of each underground/underwater shoot; without much effort, this will puncture and penetrate most liners. However, it is ideal for stabilizing the banks of lakes and rivers, and is much loved by landscapers who need to protect vulnerable river banks from erosion.

End-of-season growth can be removed and used to protect other plants against frost and wind. The slender, dried stems of this plant have numerous uses, including thatching and windbreaks: it is resistant to damp and quite strong, almost bamboo-like in appearance.

Phragmites communis can easily reach 2m (6½ft) or more, towering over, and dwarfing, any other plant in the pond. It is best kept in a non-mesh container, which will restrict the root system, preventing it from spreading and damaging the liner. There are at least two variegated cultivars of this genus: *P. australis* 'Variegatus' and *P. karka* 'Variegatus'. Although somewhat shorter, they have the same type of root system as *P. communis*, so should not be used in a lined pond.

To propagate, simply remove fresh new shoots from the root system, and pot in a heavy loam or clay medium.

Pontederia cordata
Pickerel weed

True aquatic; Hardy herbaceous perennial

Natural habitat
Wetlands, borders and margins of natural bodies of water

Ideal conditions
Water, shallow to 15cm (6in)

Ideal planting depth
0–15cm (0–6in) below water

Light requirements
Full sun to dappled shade

Soil preference
Heavy loam to clay

Normal height
60–80cm (2–2½ft)

Flower type
Small single flowers clustered on a poker-like spike

Flower colour
Sky blue

Flowering time
Late summer

Propagation
By seed or division of creeping, rhizome-like root

Particulars

Another plant from North America, this beautiful and striking true aquatic is one plant that every pond should have.

Dark green, glossy, heart-shaped leaves are borne on lighter coloured stems that rise out of the water, growing steadily to a height of 60cm (2ft) or more. The more nutrients and sunshine this plant has, the taller and larger it will grow – perhaps up to 90cm (3ft). Its unusual, sky-blue flower clusters appear at the top of 60cm (2ft) spikes during the late summer. A mature plant will produce five or six flower stems lasting, in total, two to three weeks.

The plant is non-invasive, having a relatively slow, compact, clump-forming habit. This makes it ideal for any pond, large or small. The subspecies *Pontederia cordata alba* is white flowering. *Pontederia lanceolata*, another blue-flowered species, has elongated, lance-shaped leaves, with the same dark green, glossy appearance. All behave in the same manner.

The foliage has a very high cellulose content and should be removed as it dies off, to avoid pollution; because cellulose does not break down easily it remains suspended, partly decomposed. The plant appreciates a little extra food at the start of the growing season, and will produce lush foliage as a result.

Seed should be collected in the autumn, when ripe, planted directly into wet soil, and left outdoors. Seedlings will appear early the following summer. When large enough to handle, these should be pricked out into a heavy, loam-based medium and kept wet, in a sunny spot. They will be ready for the pond the following season. The division of roots is a simple matter of teasing apart mature clumps – these part fairly readily. Plant up and place in the pond straight away.

Ranunculus flammula
Lesser spearwort

True aquatic; Hardy herbaceous perennial

Natural habitat
Wetlands and borders of natural bodies of water

Ideal conditions
Shallow water

Ideal planting depth
0–5cm (0–2in) below water

Light requirements
Full sun to dappled shade

Soil preference
Heavy loam to clay

Normal height
15–20cm (6–8in)

Flower type
Single, buttercup-like

Flower colour
Golden-yellow

Flowering time
Early summer

Propagation
By stem cuttings or seed

Particulars
Ranunculus flammula can become a sprawling, untidy plant in most situations. The natural habit of its initially erect, cylindrical stems is to flop over and sprawl. They spread over the surface of the water to reproduce vegetatively, frequently establishing new plants from each leaf node. The stems are often flushed with red, offsetting the dark green, spear-shaped leaves. Golden-yellow, buttercup-like flowers appear in profusion from early to midsummer, with a flowering period lasting up to two weeks.

Old plants, past their best, should be trimmed right back to encourage fresh new growth. Additional food is not required; this plant does very nicely without any help. So saying, it is ideal for a wildlife pond, providing plenty of cover.

Pollinated flowers produce clusters of small, mace-like seed heads all over the tangled mass of stem. Collect these when ripe and store until the following spring. Plant out in late spring, in a moist situation where they will receive maximum light. They will germinate relatively quickly and be ready for pricking out in about six weeks. However, for general purposes there is no need to go to such lengths. By harvesting the young plants formed by the plant's naturally multiplying behaviour, you can obtain all you'll ever need.

97

Ranunculus lingua
Greater spearwort

True aquatic; Hardy herbaceous perennial

Natural habitat
Wetland and marshland, margins of natural bodies of water

Ideal conditions
Shallow water

Ideal planting depth
0–15cm (0–6in) below water

Light requirements
Full sun

Soil preference
Heavy loam to clay

Normal height
70–90cm (2½–3ft)

Flower type
Single, buttercup-like

Flower colour
Golden-yellow

Flowering time
Midsummer

Propagation
By root cuttings or seed

Particulars
Ranunculus lingua, although quite a handsome plant, is not one for the smaller garden pond: it possesses a vigorous stoloniferous, creeping rootstock that can and will colonize large areas.

Under ideal conditions the plant can easily reach heights of 90cm (3ft) or more, requiring large containers to support it.

The red-tinged, hollow stems sport long, dark green, lanceolate leaves – some 15–20cm (6–8in) long – at regular intervals along their length. Large, buttercup-like flowers appear at the top of the stems in midsummer, opening up to about 5cm (2in) in diameter.

Remove all old, dying or dead leaves and stems to avoid pollution. Should stems break and fall into the water, they will root from the leaf nodes; care should be taken to remove these or your pond will soon fill with this one plant. The plant does not require additional food at any time.

Propagation is accomplished by potting 10cm (4in) lengths, or trimmings, of the thick, fleshy, white growing points. These are usually found below the underwater soil.

Pollinated flowers produce pretty, light green, mace-like seed heads that ripen slowly, turning light brown as they do so. Collect seeds as soon as they are ripe and plant immediately, in moist soil. Leave out all winter and the seeds will germinate from late spring to early summer. However, growing from seed is rarely necessary, as this plant is so prolific.

Rumex sanguineus
Blood-veined dock

Hardy herbaceous perennial

Natural habitat
Natural wetlands and marsh land

Ideal conditions
Moist to wet soil

Ideal planting depth
2.5cm (1in) above to 2.5cm (1in) below water

Light requirements
Full sun to partial shade

Soil preference
Not fussy

Normal height
Foliage: 15–20cm (6–8in)
Flower panicle: 50–60cm (18–24ft)

Flower type
Single, small

Flower colour
White

Flowering time
Early summer

Propagation
By seed

Particulars

This plant is grown for its very attractive foliage – a bright, light green, heavily veined with dark, blood red lines. En masse it puts out a very good show of colour in late spring and early summer.

The tiny flowers appear in early summer on a relatively tall, branched panicle. These rapidly turn into elongated clusters of small, red-tinged seeds; if you don't want blood-veined dock all over the garden, remove these as soon as they form.

Remove the first flush of foliage once it is past its best; this will encourage new, lush growth to replace the old, decaying leaves and help maintain the desirable foliage colour.

While this plant is self-sufficient under normal circumstances, a small amount of additional food, in the form of bone meal, will produce larger, lusher growth.

Should you wish to grow more, simply sprinkle seed into a tray of moist soil and let nature take its course; with this plant you can be sure it will.

Sagittaria species (*Sagittaria japonica* shown below)
Arrowhead

True aquatics; Hardy herbaceous perennials

Natural habitat
Shallow margins of natural bodies of water

Ideal conditions
Shallow water

Ideal planting depth
2.5–15cm (1–6in) below water

Light requirements
Full sun

Soil preference
Heavy loam to clay

Normal height
60cm (2ft)

Flower type
Three-petalled, single

Flower colour
White

Flowering time
Summer

Propagation
By tuber

Particulars

All the sagittaria species are popular and attractive, even regarded by some as architectural in form. They include *Sagittaria japonica* (syn. *Sagittaria sagittifolia* 'Flore Pleno') (Japanese arrowhead), and *Sagittaria saggittifolia* (common arrowhead) which is the most commonly found. Both are true aquatics and have the same behavioural characteristics. *Sagittaria japonica* has white petals with yellow-green centres whilst *S. saggittifolia* has purple-black centres; no doubt you will find that they are frequently confused.

Both varieties have root systems that produce new tubers via a stoloniferous rootstock. *Sagittaria saggittifolia* is the most vigorous and can colonize quite large areas if not watched. *Sagittaria japonica* has attractive leaves supported on long, pale green stems that extend to 60cm (2ft) or more. All sagittarias sport arrow-shaped leaves, albeit in slightly differing forms; the name sagittaria is from the latin, *sagitta*, meaning arrow. The flowers, though quite attractive en masse, are not the principle reason for growing *S. saggittifolia* – it is a foliage plant. However, the double flowers of *S. japonica* make this beautiful plant well worth the effort.

A word of caution; ducks love the tubers of these plants. If you have ducks in the vicinity, you will have considerable difficulty in retaining your plant for long: they will seek them out and consume them voraciously.

These plants appreciate extra food in spring, in the form of a little bone meal, producing larger flowers and stronger foliage as a result.

To propagate, merely take off some of the larger, bulb-like tubers, pot in good, heavy soil, and return to the water. New plants will soon appear.

Saururus cernuus
Lizard's tail/swamp lily/water dragon

Hardy herbaceous perennial

Natural habitat
Marshland

Ideal conditions
Moist to wet ground

Ideal planting depth
0–5cm (0–2in) below water

Light requirements
Full sun

Soil preference
Not fussy, but does not appreciate a high peat content

Normal height
30–60cm (1–2ft)

Flower type
Single, clustered on a pendulous spike

Flower colour
Creamy white

Flowering time
Midsummer

Propagation
By division of roots

Particulars
This North American plant has an unusual flower, from which it gets its name. The long, dangling flower spike – which can reach up to 10cm (4in) – consists of a multitude of tiny, creamy white, single flowers that appear as one. The spike is slightly 'S' shaped, and somewhat reminiscent of a lizard's tail in form. The leaves are cordate (heart-shaped) and light green with slightly paler but emphasized veining along their length. The branching stems are pale yellow-green and a little woody; they often reach 60cm (2ft), and sometimes a little more.

The plant has a creeping, fleshy, white, stoloniferous root system. This is not over-vigorous and is relatively easy to control with the occasional trim. The plant does appreciate small amounts of bone meal in early spring. Other than this, general care involves simply ensuring that the plant does not dry out, and removing decaying and dead leaves as required.

Propagation is achieved by removing a length of root of about 10cm (4in), and potting in good heavy loam, in warm, sunny, moist conditions.

101

Schizostylis coccinea
Kaffir lily

Hardy herbaceous perennial

Natural habitat
Damp, herbaceous borders

Ideal conditions
Damp ground

Ideal planting depth
5cm (2in) above to 2.5cm (1in) below water

Light requirements
Full sun

Soil preference
Heavy loam

Normal height
60–75cm (2–2½ft)

Flower type
Gladiolus, trumpet-like

Flower colour
Pink, red or white

Flowering time
Late summer

Propagation
By division of root-bulblet cluster

Particulars

This species has a number of cultivars ranging from red, through pink to white. All flower at the same time – late summer. The flowers and foliage are very similar to a gladiolus, though somewhat smaller; they usually reach only 60cm (2ft) or so. The flower stem appears from the blue-green, sword-shaped leaves, to open with a succession of up to 12 beautiful flowers, one after the other.

Although originally from the herbaceous border, this plant has been found to enjoy a wet environment. Its late-flowering habit is another bonus: it flowers when most other plants around the pond are finished and starting to die back.

It is best to remove old flower stems when flowering is over: this allows the plant to regain strength before the winter.

Providing a kaffir lily is kept from freezing, it will continue to thrive for many years. It is worth lowering the plant beneath ice level before the onset of the severest weather.

Propagation is accomplished by removing the young bulblets to be found amongst the root mass. Pot these in good soil with a little bone meal, keep moist and warm, and young plants will soon emerge. It will take at least another year before these flower.

Schoenoplectus lacustris subsp. *tabernaemontani* 'Zebrinus' (syn. *Scirpus tabernaemontani* 'Zebrinus')

Zebra rush

True aquatic; Hardy herbaceous perennial

Natural habitat
Muddy margins of natural bodies of water

Ideal conditions
Moist to wet ground

Ideal planting depth
0–10cm (0–4in) below water

Light requirements
Full sun to partial shade

Soil preference
Heavy loam to clay

Normal height
90–110cm (3–4ft)

Flower type
No significant flower; pubescent seed pod

Flower colour
No significant flower; brown seed head

Flowering time
No significant flower; seed heads in midsummer

Propagation
By division of roots

Particulars
One of many plants belonging to the genus schoenoplectus, this cultivar is, basically, a white form of the common bulrush, *Schoenoplectus lacustris*. It can reach heights of 2m (6½ft) or more. The slender stem, cylindrical and hollow, has horizontal bands of green breaking up the white background. They are quite delicate and easily succumb to strong winds and mishandling, bending and looking unsightly, but a clean surgical cut just below the damaged area will restore them.

The plant has a tendency to revert to the basic, all-green stem of *S. lacustris*; if this occurs, all affected stems should be removed as soon as they appear. The white background does tend to fade a little in high summer but moving the plant to a more shaded spot will reduce this colour loss. Food, in the form of bone meal, is welcomed by this plant, which responds by producing beautifully marked, lush growth, in quantity. Old growth should be removed as and when required.

Propagation is a matter of dividing the tough, wiry root system. This is best achieved with a sharp knife, cutting straight down through the root mass. A mature plant will provide enough material for several new plants. These should be kept in shallow water, in a warm sunny spot, until established. They can then be placed around the pond.

103

Typha angustifolia
Slender reed mace/slender cat's tail

True aquatic; Hardy herbaceous perennial

Natural habitat
Shallow margins of natural bodies of water

Ideal conditions
Shallow water

Ideal planting depth
5cm (2in) above to 15cm (6in) below water

Light requirements
Full sun to partial shade

Soil preference
Heavy loam to clay

Normal height
1.5m (5ft)

Flower type
Spadix, cigar-like

Flower colour
Brown

Flowering time
Summer

Propagation
By cuttings or division of creeping root system

Particulars
Typha angustifolia is one of the most attractive of the more commonly available reed maces. Its graceful, slender, blue-green leaves frame the tall, chocolate-tipped flower stems throughout the summer. The leaves will die back in winter but the woody flower stem remains statuesque, looking very pretty when covered with frost.

This is not a plant for the small or lined pond as it possesses a very strong and vigorous, stoloniferous root system armed with a sharp growing point. This point is quite capable of penetrating most liners, especially if it has nowhere else to grow – do beware. The first signs of trouble will be its appearance in the garden alongside the pond. It is unlikely that the pond will start to leak until the root system dies back, by which time it is far too late to do anything.

Typha angustifolia is best suited to large, natural ponds and lakes and is quite useful in aiding the stabilization of river banks, as the roots form a dense mat just below the surface.

Old foliage should be removed before winter, to avoid unnecessary pollution. The plant will not require feeding at any time

Propagation is simplicity itself; just remove a length of root system that has a healthy growing tip and some roots, pot this in heavy loam or clay and place in the water, barely submerged.

Typha latifolia
Reed mace/cat's tail

True aquatic; Hardy herbaceous perennial

Natural habitat
Shallow margins of natural bodies of water

Ideal conditions
Shallow water

Ideal planting depth
5cm (2in) above to 15cm (6in) below water

Light requirements
Full sun to partial shade

Soil preference
Heavy loam to clay

Normal height
2m (6½ft)

Flower type
Spadix, cigar-like

Flower colour
Brown

Flowering time
Summer

Propagation
By cuttings or division of creeping root system

Particulars
Typha latifolia is big in every way. The broad, blue-green leaves can reach considerable heights and as they do so, they frame the taller flower stems, tipped with dark brown, throughout the summer. The leaves die back in winter but the woody flower stems remain throughout the winter, looking quite attractive when covered with frost.

This is not a plant for the small or lined pond as it possesses a very strong and vigorous, stoloniferous root system armed with a sharp growing point. This point is quite capable of penetrating most liners, especially if it has nowhere else to grow – do beware. The first signs of trouble will be its appearance in the garden alongside the pond. It is unlikely that the pond will start to leak until the root system dies back, by which time it is far too late to do anything. The plant is best suited to large, natural ponds and lakes. It is useful in aiding the stabilization of river banks, as the massive root system forms a tough, dense, almost raft-like mat just below the surface.

Old foliage should be removed before winter, to avoid unnecessary pollution. The plant will not require feeding at any time.

Propagation is simplicity itself; just remove a length of root system that has a healthy growing tip and some roots, pot in heavy loam or clay, and place in the water, just submerged.

105

Typha minima
Miniature reed mace

True aquatic; Hardy herbaceous perennial

Natural habitat
Shallow margins of natural bodies of water

Ideal conditions
Shallow water

Ideal planting depth
5cm (2in) above to 10cm (4in) below water

Light requirements
Full sun to partial shade

Soil preference
Heavy loam to clay

Normal height
50–60cm (1½–2ft)

Flower type
Globe like

Flower colour
Brown

Flowering time
Summer

Propagation
By cuttings or division of creeping root system

Particulars
Typha minima is a handy little plant, often used in small ponds. Its globular seed head is considerably different from the cigar-shaped spadix of its near cousins. The leaves are very slender, almost a miniature version of *T. angustifolia* leaves. However, when it comes to the root system, it is typical of the genus, possessing a strong growing point that does not always stop for pond liners.

The root system is more woody than others in the family but just as prolific. Some care is needed if you keep this plant. The first signs of trouble will be young shoots appearing in the garden alongside the pond; it is unlikely that the pond will start to leak until the root system dies back, well after the damage has been done.

This plant is best left in natural ponds and lakes where it can do little harm. However, it is quite attractive, and more suited to the garden pond than its cousins because of its diminutive size. If some care is taken, it is fine. Placing an additional liner between the root system and the pond liner will protect the pond liner from the sharp, pointed roots.

Old foliage should be removed before winter, to avoid unnecessary pollution. The plant will not require feeding at any time.

Propagation is simplicity itself; just remove a length of root system that has a healthy growing tip and some roots, pot in heavy loam or clay and place in the water, just submerged.

Veronica beccabunga
Brooklime

True aquatic; Hardy herbaceous perennial

Natural habitat
Marshy ground to shallow water

Ideal conditions
Shallow water

Ideal planting depth
0–5cm (0–2in) below water

Light requirements
Full sun to partial shade

Soil preference
Not too fussy

Normal height
15cm (6in)

Flower type
Small, single

Flower colour
Blue

Flowering time
Early summer

Propagation
By stem cuttings

Particulars

Brooklime is a low, scrambling, aquatic plant that has the ability to hide a multitude of sins, such as unsightly exposed pond liner around the edges of ponds. The dark green, elliptic leaves are borne in profusion along branching, lighter green stems. The pretty, royal-blue flowers appear on short, branching stalks in early summer, to fade and die off within the space of a week or two. The stems can reach lengths of 2m (6ft) or more, blanketing large areas. Their aeriel root systems do a wonderful job of pond cleaning, consuming excess plant food that algae would otherwise utilize. Like watercress, brooklime can be a poor man's water clearance plant, it is capable of such prolific growth.

The plant can become untidy if it is not kept trimmed. Pinching out the tips of the long stems will encourage more side growth. Fully hardy, the leaves remain until quite late into autumn. The majority of the growth should then be removed, to avoid needless pollution.

Propagation is achieved by planting up trimmings and keeping them moist for a week or two, after which they can be placed in the pond.

Zantedeschia aethiopica
Arum lily

Hardy herbaceous perennial

Natural habitat
Damp, shady areas

Ideal conditions
Moist ground with some shade

Ideal planting depth
5cm (2in) above to 10cm (4in) below water

Light requirements
Full sun to partial shade

Soil preference
Not too fussy

Normal height
Up to 1m (3ft)

Flower type
Spathe

Flower colour
Pure white

Flowering time
Early summer

Propagation
By division of roots

Particulars

The arum lily is another import from the herbaceous border and just loves water. These plants, once mature, will live quite happily in the pond with 15cm (6in) of water over the pot; this is, in fact, the best way to protect the plant against ice damage in the winter.

The large, almost arrowhead-shaped leaves are borne on long stalks, reaching up to 1m (3ft) in height in ideal conditions. A mature plant can bear as many as six to eight flowers in one season. This is not a plant to be missed, for the pond or garden.

The foliage has a high cellulose content and should be removed as soon as it starts to fail: as cellulose does not break down easily, pollution can be a problem if some care is not taken. Remove old flowers as they die back to encourage more to show. Additional food is appreciated by this plant, as it consumes vast quantities in order to maintain its considerable mass of lush foliage.

To propagate, remove the plant from its container and shake off most of the soil to expose the root mass; here you will find young plants and bulblets that can be removed and potted, then grown on.

ABOUT THE AUTHOR

Bernard Sleeman first became interested in aquatic plants in the late 1960s whilst living in the Far East. On his return to England, with his quest for knowledge about why certain aquatic plants grow where they do and what their role is, his budding interest developed into a part-time hobby. The information he gathered gave him an invaluable insight into pond and plant health and he became increasingly involved with aquatic plants. This led him into their mass propagation, and engendered a special interest in new species and varieties. Bernard has now built up an appreciable private collection of waterlilies.

INDEX

Page numbers in **bold** refer to illustrations

S

Sagittaria (arrowhead) 100
  japonica (Japanese arrowhead) **100**
  sagittifolia (common arrowhead) 100
salad crops 20
salads 90
Saururus cernuus (lizard's tail/swamp
  lily/water dragon) **101**
Schizostylis coccinea (kaffir lily) **102**
Schoenoplectus lacustris
  tabernaemontani 'Zebrinus' (zebra
  rush) **103**
seasonal change 8
sedge grass (*Carex pseudocyperus*) **47**
Siberia 69
Siberian flag (*Iris sibirica*) **69**
slender cat's tail (*Typha angustifolia*)
  104, 106
slender reed mace (*Typha
  angustifolia*) **104**, 106
slugs 75
snails 6
soil conditions 15–16
South Africa 37
southern France 74
sowing seeds **23**
stabilizing river banks 95, 104
stem cuttings 27
stick grubs 20
stoloniferous stems, dividing **26**

striped water grass (*Glyceria
  aquatica variegata*) **56**
submerged aquatics 91
submerged plants 11
sulphur dioxide 16
swamp lily (*Saururus cernuus*) **101**
sweet flag (*Acorus calamus*) **32**
sweet galingale (*Cyperus longus*) **51**
systemic insecticides 21

T

terrestrial plants 13
tip cuttings 57
toxic pond 9
trace elements 16
tubers, dividing **29**
twisted bamboo 73
Typha
  angustifolia (slender reed
   mace/slender cat's tail) **104**, 106
  latifolia (reed mace/cat's tail) **105**
  minima (miniature reed mace) **106**

U

umbrella grass (*Cyperus
  involucratus*) **50**
unpleasant smell 78, 79
unsightly areas 49, 74, 80, 107

TITLES AVAILABLE FROM

GMC Publications

BOOKS

WOODCARVING

Beginning Woodcarving	*GMC Publications*
Carving Architectural Detail in Wood: The Classical Tradition	*Frederick Wilbur*
Carving Birds & Beasts	*GMC Publications*
Carving the Human Figure: Studies in Wood and Stone	*Dick Onians*
Carving Nature: Wildlife Studies in Wood	*Frank Fox-Wilson*
Carving on Turning	*Chris Pye*
Decorative Woodcarving	*Jeremy Williams*
Elements of Woodcarving	*Chris Pye*
Essential Woodcarving Techniques	*Dick Onians*
Lettercarving in Wood: A Practical Course	*Chris Pye*
Making & Using Working Drawings for Realistic Model Animals	*Basil F. Fordham*
Power Tools for Woodcarving	*David Tippey*
Relief Carving in Wood: A Practical Introduction	*Chris Pye*
Understanding Woodcarving in the Round	*GMC Publications*
Useful Techniques for Woodcarvers	*GMC Publications*
Woodcarving: A Foundation Course	*Zoë Gertner*
Woodcarving for Beginners	*GMC Publications*
Woodcarving Tools, Materials & Equipment (New Edition)	*Chris Pye*

WOODTURNING

Adventures in Woodturning	*David Springett*
Bert Marsh: Woodturner	*Bert Marsh*
Bowl Turning Techniques Masterclass	*Tony Boase*
Colouring Techniques for Woodturners	*Jan Sanders*
Contemporary Turned Wood: New Perspectives in a Rich Tradition	*Ray Leier, Jan Peters & Kevin Wallace*
The Craftsman Woodturner	*Peter Child*
Decorating Turned Wood: The Maker's Eye	*Liz & Michael O'Donnell*
Decorative Techniques for Woodturners	*Hilary Bowen*
Illustrated Woodturning Techniques	*John Hunnex*
Intermediate Woodturning Projects	*GMC Publications*
Keith Rowley's Woodturning Projects	*Keith Rowley*
Making Screw Threads in Wood	*Fred Holder*
Turned Boxes: 50 Designs	*Chris Stott*
Turning Green Wood	*Michael O'Donnell*
Turning Pens and Pencils	*Kip Christensen & Rex Burningham*
Useful Woodturning Projects	*GMC Publications*
Woodturning: Bowls, Platters, Hollow Forms, Vases, Vessels, Bottles, Flasks, Tankards, Plates	*GMC Publications*
Woodturning: A Foundation Course (New Edition)	*Keith Rowley*
Woodturning: A Fresh Approach	*Robert Chapman*
Woodturning: An Individual Approach	*Dave Regester*
Woodturning: A Source Book of Shapes	*John Hunnex*
Woodturning Jewellery	*Hilary Bowen*
Woodturning Masterclass	*Tony Boase*
Woodturning Techniques	*GMC Publications*

WOODWORKING

UPHOLSTERY

TOYMAKING

DOLLS' HOUSES AND MINIATURES

CRAFTS

GARDENING

PHOTOGRAPHY

An Essential Guide to Bird Photography	*Steve Young*
Field Guide to Landscape Photography	*Peter Watson*
Light in the Landscape: A Photographer's Year	*Peter Watson*
Outdoor Photography Portfolio	*GMC Publications*
Photographing Fungi in the Field	*George McCarthy*
Photography for the Naturalist	*Mark Lucock*
Viewpoints from *Outdoor Photography*	*GMC Publications*
Where and How to Photograph Wildlife	*Peter Evans*

VIDEOS

Drop-in and Pinstuffed Seats	*David James*
Stuffover Upholstery	*David James*
Elliptical Turning	*David Springett*
Woodturning Wizardry	*David Springett*
Turning Between Centres: The Basics	*Dennis White*
Turning Bowls	*Dennis White*
Boxes, Goblets and Screw Threads	*Dennis White*
Novelties and Projects	*Dennis White*
Classic Profiles	*Dennis White*
Twists and Advanced Turning	*Dennis White*
Sharpening the Professional Way	*Jim Kingshott*
Sharpening Turning & Carving Tools	*Jim Kingshott*
Bowl Turning	*John Jordan*
Hollow Turning	*John Jordan*
Woodturning: A Foundation Course	*Keith Rowley*
Carving a Figure: The Female Form	*Ray Gonzalez*
The Router: A Beginner's Guide	*Alan Goodsell*
The Scroll Saw: A Beginner's Guide	*John Burke*

MAGAZINES

WOODTURNING ◆ WOODCARVING

FURNITURE & CABINETMAKING ◆ THE ROUTER

WOODWORKING ◆ THE DOLLS' HOUSE MAGAZINE

OUTDOOR PHOTOGRAPHY ◆ BLACK & WHITE PHOTOGRAPHY

BUSINESSMATTERS

The above represents a full list of all titles currently published or scheduled to be published.
All are available direct from the Publishers or through bookshops, newsagents and specialist retailers.
To place an order, or to obtain a complete catalogue, contact:

GMC Publications,
Castle Place, 166 High Street, Lewes, East Sussex BN7 1XU, United Kingdom
Tel: 01273 488005 Fax: 01273 478606
E-mail: pubs@thegmcgroup.com

Orders by credit card are accepted